Devil's Advocates

DEVIL'S ADVOCATES is a series of books devoted to exploring the classics of horror cinema. Contributors to the series come from the fields of teaching, academia, journalism and fiction, but all have one thing in common: a passion for the horror film and a desire to share it with the widest possible audience.

'The admirable Devil's Advocates series is not only essential – and fun – reading for the serious horror fan but should be set texts on any genre course.'
Dr Ian Hunter, Reader in Film Studies, De Montfort University, Leicester

'Auteur Publishing's new Devil's Advocates critiques on individual titles... offer bracingly fresh perspectives from passionate writers. The series will perfectly complement the BFI archive volumes.' **Christopher Fowler,** *Independent on Sunday*

'Devil's Advocates has proven itself more than capable of producing impassioned, intelligent analyses of genre cinema... quickly becoming the go-to guys for intelligent, easily digestible film criticism.' *HorrorTalk.com*

'Auteur Publishing continue the good work of giving serious critical attention to significant horror films.' *Black Static*

 DevilsAdvocatesbooks

 DevilsAdBooks

ALSO AVAILABLE IN THIS SERIES

Antichrist Amy Simmonds

Black Sunday Martyn Conterio

The Blair Witch Project Peter Turner

Cannibal Holocaust Calum Waddell

Carrie Neil Mitchell

The Company of Wolves James Gracey

The Curse of Frankenstein Marcus K. Harmes

Dead of Night Jez Conolly & David Bates

The Descent James Marriot

Halloween Murray Leeder

Ju-on: The Grudge Marisa C. Hayes

Let the Right One In Anne Billson

Macbeth Rebekah Owens

Nosferatu Cristina Massaccesi

Saw Benjamin Poole

The Shining Laura Mee

The Silence of the Lambs Barry Forshaw

Suspiria Alexandra Heller-Nicholas

The Texas Chain Saw Massacre James Rose

The Thing Jez Conolly

Witchfinder General Ian Cooper

FORTHCOMING

The Fly Emma Westwood

Frenzy Ian Cooper

In the Mouth of Madness Michael Blyth

Psychomania I.Q. Hunter & Jamie Sherry

Scream Steven West

Devil's Advocates

Don't Look Now

Jessica Gildersleeve

Acknowledgments

I am grateful to the University of Southern Queensland for research leave during the second semester of 2016, which enabled me to work on this project. My particular thanks are due to David Ellison, who set *Don't Look Now* on his course on the Gothic at Griffith University; my discussions with colleagues and students there between 2010 and 2012 helped me to formulate some of the ideas contained here. Thanks too to John Atkinson of Auteur for his interest and belief in the project.

Although I had not anticipated it, much of this book was written while I was expecting my first child. That experience has given me a new perspective on the parental anxiety I explore here, and I thank my (at the time of writing, unborn and unnamed) son for those insights.

Dedication

For Adam and the little one.

First published in 2017 by
Auteur, 24 Hartwell Crescent, Leighton Buzzard LU7 1NP
www.auteur.co.uk
Copyright © Auteur 2017

Series design: Nikki Hamlett at Cassels Design
Set by Cassels Design www.casselsdesign.co.uk
Printed and bound in Great Britain

All rights reserved. No part of this publication may be reproduced in any material form (including photocopying or storing in any medium by electronic means and whether or not transiently or incidentally to some other use of this publication) without the permission of the copyright owner.

British Library Cataloguing-in-Publication Data
A catalogue record for this book is available from the British Library

ISBN paperback: 978-1-911325-48-2
ISBN ebook: 978-1-911325-49-9

Contents

List of Figures vi

Introduction: Horror and Cultural Trauma in the 1970s 7

Chapter 1: Looking Again: The Critical Heritage 21

Chapter 2: Dread and the Trauma of Complicity 29

Chapter 3: *Destinerrance* and the Trauma of Misreading 45

Chapter 4: Dereliction and the Trauma of Place 57

Conclusion: *Don't Look Now* and the Cinema of Trauma 73

Bibliography 77

List of Figures

Figure 1: The original poster advertisement for *Don't Look Now*.

Figure 2: Laura and a bystander attempt to reach John through the locked gates at the film's conclusion.

Figure 3: Christine pushes a wheelbarrow in the garden while a horse gallops in the background.

Figure 4: John clutches Christine's lifeless body in horror.

Figure 5: Laura and the sisters on the funeral barge.

Figure 6: The 'lost child' is revealed as a murderous dwarf.

Figure 7: The 'bleeding' slide.

Figure 8: The hotel lobby.

Figure 9: John works on the church façade, face to face with history.

Figure 10: John falls from the scaffold inside the church.

Figure 11: The sisters' unexplained laughter.

INTRODUCTION

Horror and Cultural Trauma in the 1970s

Nicolas Roeg's *Don't Look Now* (1973) has been called 'a ghost story for adults' (Moore 1983, p. 93). Certainly, in contrast to the more explicitly violent and bloodthirsty horror films of the 1970s – perhaps most prominently, *The Exorcist* (dir. William Friedkin, 1973), *The Texas Chain Saw Massacre* (dir. Tobe Hooper, 1974), *The Omen* (dir. Richard Donner, 1976), *Carrie* (dir. Brian De Palma, 1976) and *Halloween* (dir. John Carpenter, 1978) – *Don't Look Now* seems of an entirely different order. Yet, in its final, terrible scene of John Baxter's death and, too, in his daughter's accidental drowning, and her parents' desperate simultaneous recoil from her death and pursuit of her ghost, *Don't Look Now* is horrific at every turn. This book argues for *Don't Look Now* as a particular kind of horror film, one which depends utterly on the narrative of trauma – on the horror of unknowing, of seeing too late, and of the failures of paternal authority and responsibility. It *is* a 'ghost story for adults', to be sure, but more than this, it is a horror film for 1970s Britain: a nation in social, economic and political turmoil, and a nation in which certainty has been lost. The purpose of this chapter is to situate *Don't Look Now* within the landscape of 1970s cinema in general, and 1970s horror cinema in particular, as well as to establish the significance of specific kinds of cultural trauma in *Don't Look Now* as a horror film of that decade.

Despite a recent *Guardian* poll in which *Don't Look Now* was named the third best horror film of all time (Billson 2010), and the fact that it was among the top twenty films of the 1970s, as well as the 'top grossing British film of 1974' (Street 2009, p. 95), it is an often-cited fact that although *Don't Look Now* was released in the same year as William Friedkin's *The Exorcist*, it has never enjoyed the same critical or popular attention as its counterpart. Similarly, one might compare the enduring popularity of a number of other prominent horror films of the late 1960s and 1970s and even into the early 1980s, such as *The Omen*, *Rosemary's Baby* (dir. Roman Polanski, 1968) and *The Shining* (dir. Stanley Kubrick, 1980), all of which also feature children as a key component of the plot and the source of fear. The reason for the distinction may lie in a number of factors, although each offers its own caveat: *Don't Look Now*'s greater restraint with regard to violence

– albeit its final scene is as visceral as any in the other films; its treatment of sexuality – although the love scene between the couple was so intimate that it attracted the censor's attention; or even in its maximum classification rating in both the United States and the United Kingdom.

What I want to suggest, however, is that *Don't Look Now* offers up a different kind of horror than most other films of the period. Horror films are often, like Westerns or crime texts, noted for their repetitive patterns and the recognisable tropes of genre. However, *Don't Look Now* does not adhere to those tropes – as Darrell Moore long ago noted, this is a distinctly adult horror film. As such, this study works to position *Don't Look Now* within a discourse of traumatic and anxious narratives primarily existing in literary texts around mid-century. In this context, it represents a cross over or a hinge between literature and film of the 1970s, and the ways in which the 'women's ghost story' or 'uncanny story' turns the horror film into a cultural commentary on the failures of the modern family. Rather than fear deriving purely from the chase, the threat of a psychotic killer, an unfamiliar environment, or a betrayal of innocence – although, again, the film does contain all of these tropes – *Don't Look Now*'s horror finds its source in being wrong, in making mistakes, in seeing or knowing too late. Indeed, whereas the slasher film of the 1970s creates the pleasure of horror in its repetition, in the audience's knowledge that death is to come but remains 'in the dark', as it were, only as to when and how it will arrive, *Don't Look Now*'s horror is precisely the horror of *not* knowing, of not recognising a threat as such, but seeing it as familiar, domestic, safe. The horror of *Don't Look Now* is the horror of misreading, and John's shock at both story and film's end – narrated in the former as, 'Oh God … what a bloody silly way to die …' (Du Maurier 2006, p. 55) – offers up the humiliation and shock of that too-late revelation. This is not the horror of being chased, but of not even realising that one was being pursued; it is not the horror of discovering a murderer, but of realising that one's 'child' is the killer; it is not the horror of witnessing the death of a loved one, but the knowledge that one should have prevented it. It is the horror of not seeing or knowing what one should have seen or known all along.

Horror Cinema in the 1970s

Don't Look Now might be understood in the context of the history of Gothic narratives, exposing and satirising the tropes of that genre and the ways in which the film's characters read or misread those signs. It is precisely in the gap between such readings and misreadings, between knowing and unknowing, that Gothic texts produce what Angela Carter identifies as 'unease' – what she sees to be their 'singular moral function' (cited in Cavallaro 2002, p. 2), since such unease might be seen to produce or instigate social or individual change. This unease remains even after a narrative has concluded – '[e]ven narratives which round off their plots by declaring one party triumphant over another are inconclusive', notes Dani Cavallaro, 'even after all loose ends have apparently been tied, one is left with the feeling that a pervasive malice rules the world through ruthless self-preservation' (ibid.). One can never guard entirely against the irruption of evil, Gothic narratives claim; the inability to predict where it will next appear is part of the way in which horror is created, such that '[w]hat seems to afflict the Gothic psyche most intensely is an overarching sense of uncertainty as to whether the sources of fear lie in the past or in the future' (2002, p. 48), in the memory or the expectation of trauma. Even while, or perhaps because, both audience and characters reside in this space of uncertainty, horror films – the Gothic's twentieth-century monstrous offspring – are 'driven explicitly by curiosity' (Carroll 2003, p. 4) or epistemophilia, the desire to know – to know violence, to know torture, to know death. In the 1970s, these tropes may be particularly seen to characterise the slasher film.

The decade of the 1970s was not only 'a rich period of formal innovation throughout the film medium' more generally (Worland 2007, p. 4), it was the period in which the horror film made itself most uncannily at home. *Psycho* (dir. Alfred Hitchcock, 1960), *The Exorcist* and *Halloween*, in particular (2007, pp. 100-101), sparked the rules or tropes of the genre (later famously and explicitly called upon during the resurgence of teen horror in Wes Craven's postmodern franchise, *Scream* [1996-2011]). The sensation fiction of the 1860s had marked the period in which the Gothic came home: indeed, Carol J. Clover has argued that '[c]inema ... owes its particular success in the sensation genres ... to its unprecedented ability to manipulate point of view' (1996, p. 69). Now, horror could take place in one's own home and one's own time, rather than only on foreign shores or long ago, as had been the case until that point. So too in the 1970s the horror film shifted from the obviously alien or monstrous threats of the 1930s and '40s to the more recognisable (if exaggerated) threat of satanic cults and 'predatory sexual psychopaths stalking everyday, domestic settings' (1996, p. 87). As Alfred Hitchcock argued, murder 'belongs' in the home (cited in Cooper 2016, p. 121); for this reason, '[t]he settings of the 70s shockers are superficially attractive, suburban streets, new-fangled concrete shopping centres and local beauty spots, ponds, copses of trees but they are transformed into places where bad things happen, places as threatening as the Gothic castles of Hammer but without the dashing romance' (2016, p. 124). Moreover, whereas these earlier films, as well as the Gothic of the eighteenth to early twentieth centuries, had been possessed of a clear conservatism, in which order is restored and morality preserved at the narrative's end, in its 1970s iteration of the horror film there is no such respect for the apparently sacred order of the world, held together by church and family.[1] In these years following the Vietnam War, Jon Towlson argues, 'traditional social values became, at least to the youth audience who watched horror films, largely obsolete' (2014, p. 105). Indeed, Peter Fraser argues that the slasher film of the 1970s was influenced by the 'theatre of cruelty' (2015, pp. 156-57), and that it 'fed off something gone sick in the culture, a growing addiction to cruelty, obscenity, and death' (2015, p. 154). For Tony Magistrale, too, this return to the domestic in 1970s horror films recalls a similar shift in the nineteenth century represented by Edgar Allan Poe's work, in which the monster was not outside, but inside one's own self (2005, p. 99). In this respect, *Don't Look Now*, Magistrale suggests, follows *Psycho* in its introduction of 'a subtler – and thus all the more unsettling – brand of terror at work ... the numbing fear of an individual mind challenged and systematically unravelling' (2005, p. 105).

This rise in cinematic and narrative innovation in turn attracted 'increasingly sophisticated popular criticism that enhanced cinema's cultural prestige' (Worland 2007, p. 4). Indeed, since cinema itself is uncanny – '[t]he image we see on the screen is a kind of spectral double, the simulacrum of landscapes and townscapes filled with human beings that seem to live, to breath [sic], to talk, and yet are present only through their absence' (Prawer cited in Cherry 2009, p. 54) – horror and the 'aesthetics of cinema' are 'inherently linked' (2009, p. 54). Movies, argues David Lavery, 'are always at least potentially, horror movies' (1983, p. 49), and as such, 'the genre of the horror film ... is co-equal with the history of film itself' (1983, p. 48). The use of light and darkness, colour, sound and music, special effects, editing techniques and shots (1983, p. 55; pp. 80-86) all offer up recognised ways of reading horror as such, and of signalling or inducing certain emotions in the film's audience. Although it is subject to repetition and tropes, then, horror's very self-consciousness, its very uncanniness, means that films exploit these expectations as part of the development of fear. Indeed, if it is true that '[g]eneric pleasures are familiar pleasures' (Lipsitz 1998, p. 208), then it is precisely by troubling those generic boundaries that horror films map unfamiliarity within their sociocultural context, so that 'problems of the present … intrude' upon this 'seemingly fixed' genre' (ibid.). In the late 1970s, in particular, horror cinema was paid particular attention in the context of second-wave feminism and psychoanalysis (Cherry 2009, p. 95). Horror's very multiplicity – including the Gothic, the supernatural, psychological horror, slashers, and body horror (Worland 2007, p. 3, pp. 5-6) – and its malleability mark out some of the ways in which it responds to cultural anxieties. In fact, such responses are part of the pleasure of watching for its audience (Cherry 2009, p. 169).

Brigid Cherry (2009) has argued that different kinds of horror films appear at different points in history, 'in response to social anxieties about violence, family breakdown, the war on terror, climate change, and so forth' (2009, p. 19). Indeed, such issues, Cherry adds, 'contribute to the genre's continuation' (2009, p. 11). In both Britain and the United States, horror films in the 1970s became a means of exploring and expressing such social concerns, including, Paul Newman has detailed, a troubled economy, as well as racial, cultural and sexual changes (2010, pp. 11-12; see also Harper 2010, p. 24; Higson 1994; Street 2009, p. 92). Although, then, the 1970s has 'been seen as an era of decline for British cinema' (Shail cited in Newman 2010, p. 12), its 'fragmentation and transformation' (2010, p. 16) is actually best understood in the horror films of the decade. That is, as Peri Bradley puts it, '[t]he angst and anguish that reverberated through a society that found itself in a state of such flux and uncertainty, yet was unable to fully articulate this in a politically correct manner, found an outlet for expression in the most politically incorrect of forms, the horror film' (2010, p. 123). In Britain, horror films produced around mid-century often find an affiliation with the crime narratives so popular in the period during and just following the First World War. During this 'Golden Age' of crime fiction, writers such as Agatha Christie popularised narratives of murder and other crime which nevertheless excised any reference to violence or corporeal damage. A number of Christie's novels were adapted for film during this period, suggesting, Sarah Street argues, 'the nostalgic desire for the more ordered world ... where crime does not pay, poverty and deprivation do not exist and narrative closure is always assured with devastating aplomb' (2009, p. 101). But in the 1970s, a kind of dystopian attitude associated 'with terrorist bombings and strikes, power cuts, rising crime and growth of the far right' meant that, as Ian Cooper notes, 'it's not hard to see 70s Britain as a breeding ground for violent horror fantasies' (2016, p. 115). But violence was not the only point of horror in films of this period. In the context of a nation horrified by the Vietnam War (Worland 2007, p. 96), horror and crime, or the psychological thriller, marked an interest in the 'horror of madness' (Newman 2002, p. 71), rather than the more morally simple violence of the slasher film which was popular in the US.[2] Similarly, British horror films of the period drew on the occult and the supernatural; the witch figure, in particular, signals 'male anxiety and/or female power' (Hunt 2002, p. 89), associated with what Towlson refers to as the 'conservative forces at play in Britain' at the time, including 'the suspension of capital punishment, the legalisation of abortion, decriminalisation of homosexuality and the relaxation of divorce laws' (2014, p. 92). Although it is true that the Gothic and its descendant, horror, is a remarkably conservative genre, that point was contested in 1970s horror films; as Robin Wood has shown, during this decade, on both sides of the Atlantic, 'the most intense and aggressive horror films were more or less directly reflecting the radical momentum of the counter-culture and social liberation movements for blacks, women, and gays' (Worland 2007, p. 21).

In this sense, *Don't Look Now* is notable for its restraint, or what Street refers to as 'a more sophisticated blend of horror and thriller with Italian locations' (2009, p. 94). Instead, the film is recognised for 'Roeg's editing ... and cinematographic skills rather than the campy kitsch and sexploitation which characterised many horror films of the 1970s' (2009, p. 95). In part, this highly aesthetic style is also a function of Roeg's attempts to pass the film through the British and American censors of the period. John Trevelyan, Secretary of the British Board of Film Censors during the 1960s and into the early 1970s, was particularly concerned about any connections made between horror and sex (cited in Barber 2009, pp. 356-57) which had been popularised during the 1960s (Tudor 1989, p. 56). Although Roeg did use montage effects in the infamous sex scene between John and Laura in order to remove the offensive 'humping', as it was termed by the American censor, the film was given an X rating in the UK (suitable only for those aged over eighteen), and an R rating in the US (viewers under seventeen to be accompanied by an adult). For this reason, too, then, the film was positioned in an undeniably 'adult' category, outside of the popular teen horror or slasher films which later dominated the decade. Instead, *Don't Look Now* is an example of what Steven Schneider refers to as 'cinematic horror' (cited in Cherry 2009, p. 7), aimed at an audience which differed from the typical young, male audience of horror films – an audience which 'might include female, older, and high-brow audience segments' (ibid.). In a decade in which the British film industry was suffering from the loss of American financial support and a decrease in a cinema-going audience (Higson 1994, p. 216), it was one of only a few successful British-European co-productions (Barber 2012, p. 16), more artistic and high culture in its aims, and set apart from its horror counterparts in doing so.

HORROR CINEMA AND PSYCHOANALYSIS

Horror films are often associated with monsters – vampires, zombies, psychotic killers. Indeed, David J. Russell even refers to horror movies as 'monster movies' (1998, p. 234). The term 'monster' derives from the Latin *monere*, a warning; in horror films, the monster 'stands in for social disorder and rampant desire', for 'the breakdown and failure of repression' (1998, p. 237), and any changes in the ways in which monsters are represented can be linked to 'social and cultural attitudes towards aspects of identity' (Cherry 2009, p. 176). That is, as Andrew Tudor has explained:

> While the horror movies of the first three decades revolve around the twin poles of science and supernature, and their monsters threaten us largely, though not entirely, from 'outside', the second three decades bring the genre's central threat much closer to us. In these years the horror movie begins to articulate a radically different type of anxiety. The threat posed by post-1960 horror movies can be seen as expressing a profound insecurity about ourselves, and accordingly the monsters of the period are increasingly represented as part of an everyday contemporary landscape. (1989, p. 48)

Most often, it is the monster's function to disrupt the social and moral order through violence – indeed, '[i]t is the monster's body in conjunction with violence, and not the violence alone, which is the focus of the narrative disruption' (Cherry 2009, p. 29). In the 1970s, however, monstrosity primarily took the form of psychosis and madness, including supernatural possession, as in *The Exorcist*, *Rosemary's Baby* and *The Omen* (Tudor 1989, pp. 62-63). That *Don't Look Now* is unclear about precisely who is mad and/or possessed (the murderous dwarf, the psychic sisters, John, Laura, or all of them) is part of the way in which its uncanniness unsettles the audience. In fact, what is perhaps most unsettling about the monstrosity of *Don't Look Now* as a horror film is that, like Christie's stories of murder and intrigue, or like Poe's tales of psychological terror, John's 'possession', in whatever form it takes, is a figuration of 'a highly personal attack upon our being' (1989, p. 63). If sensible, sceptical John can be invaded or taken in, if the figure of the patriarch can be fooled, what hope has anyone else?

This concern about the invasion or corruption of the self, whether by a monstrous Other or by the monstrosity of the unknown corners of one's own mind, found its natural theoretical counterpart in the psychoanalytic critical discourse of the late twentieth century, and the 1970s, in particular, saw a burgeoning of psychoanalytic approaches to horror (Schneider 2004c, p. 2). The Freudian uncanny, of course, is the dominant concept applied here, describing the way in which the familiar becomes unfamiliar. The abject, too, provokes the horror of disgust, seen in the broken body, the bleeding body, the alien body, as well as the socially abject in the form of the monstrous Other. Similarly, psychoanalytic symbols of repression, like caves and cellars (Worland 2007, p. 14), recur in horror films of the period, as does the motif of the gaze, particularly in the stalker film, which often works to push 'previously submerged material to the surface' by employing the technique of aligning the point of view of the viewer and the killer, thereby disrupting the viewer's sense of moral security and seeing (rather than hiding), even delighting in, the wound (Dika 1990, pp. 20-21; see also Cherry 2009, p. 132). All of these appear in *Don't Look Now* as sites of fear and the unknown, provoking an explicit reading of the film's psychoanalytic discourse. This is not, however, a matter of mere coincidence, or of recycling the familiar, perhaps even empty tropes of horror cinema. Rather, and as this book will show, Roeg's film draws on and extends the psychoanalytic discourse in order to position *Don't Look Now* as a particular kind of horror film: the cinema of trauma. Cherry has argued that '[i]f the unconscious contains things that were repressed in order to avoid anxiety, then perhaps the activities of monsters or the traumatic events that are played out in cinematic horror are a representation of all that which is contained within the unconscious. Horror cinema could thus work as a replaying of those events and result in a working through of similar feelings of anxiety in the viewer' (2009, p. 100). Certainly, it can be argued that *Don't Look Now* plays out the horror of the unconscious, allowing the viewer to work through John and Laura's trauma and anxiety and, thereby, their own. What is perhaps more interesting, however, is to recognise the film not as a working through of trauma, but as a figuration of it: more particularly, it depicts the horrific stasis of anxiety. To hold that emotion, rather than to attempt to resolve it, is where the film becomes truly horrific.

This project thus works as a critical extension of current thinking about the relationship between horror films, psychoanalysis and contemporary cultural concerns of Britain in the 1970s, explored, for example, in Paul Newland's *Don't Look Now: British Cinema in the 1970s* (2010). More particularly, by showing that *Don't Look Now* articulates these cultural disruptions as a crisis in the family and the domestic space, and a crisis of patriarchal responsibility – or, in other words, as the traumatic undermining of certainty and authority and the law – it situates Roeg's film in the critical context of poststructuralism and affect theory, contributing not only to the critical reception of a film which has often been overlooked, but also to the broader understanding of the ethical representation of trauma in literary and film narrative. Moving beyond the recognition of the fundamental link between cinema and psychoanalysis, then, this study emphasises the way in which horror cinema provokes particular negative emotions as part of its project of cultural engagement and social responsibility. In many ways, this is not a new connection to make. Clover has argued that in addition to pornography, horror is the only genre 'specifically devoted to the arousal of bodily sensation'. The two types of films, she suggests, 'exist solely to horrify and stimulate ... and their ability to do so is the sole measure of their success' (1996, p. 69). Indeed, Cherry adds, 'horror cinema is particularly centred on its spectacle (images of cinematic horror) and the responses such spectacles are intended to create in the viewer (feelings of fear and revulsion)' (2009, p. 45). Nöel Carroll, too, defines horror cinema in terms of its ability to produce emotion; for him, these emotions are fear and disgust (1987, p. 51). It is what

Carroll terms 'art-horror', however – the high-culture, aesthetic horror cinema to which I argue *Don't Look Now* belongs – which elicits an intellectual, rather than a reflexive (shock), response through its aesthetic choices (1987, p. 53). Moreover, innovation in such choices is necessary if a film-maker is to elicit the emotion of an art-horror response, rather than simply shock (Cherry 2009, p. 4).

Anxiety is a term frequently assigned to the negative emotions produced in the viewer of the horror film. Stephen Prince asserts that the violence which is a staple of the horror film 'induce[s] anxiety because of the perceived dangers to characters in the enacted scenes' (2004a, p. 245). Tudor chooses the alternative term 'paranoia', asserting this as the dominant emotion of the early 1970s and of the horror film more generally. '[T]he horror movie itself is a paranoid form,' he argues:

> [I]t is founded on the supposition that we are constantly under threat from many directions. However, the seventies see an extension of that fear, partly conveyed in the typical narratives of the period, and partly conveyed through style and a tendency to dwell upon more overtly horrific detail. These films hit harder than their predecessors, and the threats that they present are less easily defeated – if they can be defeated at all. A straightforward list of typical seventies traits suggests the general direction of the trend: psychosis as a consequence of the psycho-sexual dynamics of the family; invasion from antagonistic and polluted nature; the relative insignificance of science; the exceptional malevolence of supernature often directed at the innocent self; predatory female sexuality; and invasion of the modern everyday by vampires, witches and demons. (1989, pp. 66-67)

Indeed, precisely because horror cinema is 'cathartic', even empathetic, Cherry argues, it is 'ideally suited to address issues of anxiety' (2009, p. 12; pp. 133-34). For Aaron Smuts and Elizabeth Cowie, following a Freudian model of the pleasure principle, although such films are often fundamentally and structurally *un*pleasurable (Cowie 2003, p. 29), their attraction lies in the fact that they provide 'a certain degree of safety not present from situations that arouse extreme distress, disgust, anger, fear, horror, misery, paranoia, and a host of other responses' (Smuts 2009, p. 53). In other words, '[t]he horror film … produc[es] images to *excite* displeasure (always associated with the visualisation/audition of a repressed content), so that it is the reversal of affect which precisely allows the recognition of the repressed image-content in the real' (Rose 1976, p. 89). Even if such emotions are inauthentic (see Tan 1996, pp. 1-3), they may still have a productive effect of this kind. For example, coming from a perspective of Christian morality, Peter Fraser has recently argued that '[h]orror is a genre designed to produce a change in the viewer', encouraging participation both in and beyond the boundaries of the film (2015, p. 135). Both Fraser and Prince point to 'the mechanics of violent death and graphic mutilation' as encouraging 'emotional responses' in the audience (Prince 2004a, p. 243). For Matt Hills, it is 'objectless anxiety, where the possessive force exceeds any one body/object and hence potentially saturates a *mise-en-scène*' which is most effective in this way. 'It may not be an accident,' he argues,

> ... that horror films sometimes thought of as 'classics' of the genre, like *Halloween* or *The Thing*, shift from object-directed emotion to objectless anxiety (and monstrous indeterminacy) in their closing frames: this movement incites audiences to leave the cinema, or switch the video/DVD off, while still in an anxious, affective mood rather than having just experienced and occurrent 'emotion.' This affect may thus linger – since it is not dependent on cognitive evaluations of an object – spilling outside the experiential time of reading/viewing the horror text, and reinforcing a sense of that text's skilful operation upon its audience .... [O]ne of the pleasures of horror may in fact lie in the transformation of experienced affect into emotion, and vice versa, as objects attach to sensation/affect, and as emotions that are introspectively refuted or detached from objects 'take off' into affective saturation of a horror text's unsettling mood or 'edgy' ambience. (2005, pp. 27-28)

Rarely, however, is anxiety explored as a psychoanalytic concept. By way of redressing this fundamental problematic in the relationship between psychoanalysis and horror cinema, the present study considers anxiety as the critical affect at the core of *Don't Look Now*'s horror.

FAMILY AND THE HORROR FILM

As cultural sites of vulnerability and possession, women have always been critical to the Gothic. Whether it is 'woman-as-monster', the so-called 'monstrous-feminine' (Creed

1993b, p. 1; p. 7), or woman as erotic object under the scopophilic gaze of the male killer and implicitly male viewer (Mulvey 1992, p. 24; pp. 27-28), women's presence in the horror film 'speaks to us more about male fears than about female desire or feminine subjectivity' (Creed 1993, p. 7). Where horror films are to do with so-called 'women's issues' or 'female problems', moreover, they are more typically termed 'thrillers' (Peirse 2015, p. 388), and revolve 'around domestic life, the family, children, self-sacrifice and the relationship between women and production vs that between women and reproduction' (Doane cited in Peirse 2015, p. 389). However, it is also the case, as Alison Peirse's analysis makes clear, that such horror films 'function as a space for women to explore emotion', and frequently the emotions to do with motherhood (2015, p. 400). Given that *Don't Look Now* offers up both of these motifs in the witch or siren figure of the red-coated dwarf and the abject misery of the childless mother, it might be tempting to read the film in these terms. However, it is also true that the film situates these emotions typically associated with women and motherhood with men and fatherhood, or with parenthood more generally, thereby establishing a tension between the horror of patriarchal failure and the potential resolutions offered by maternal mourning. In refusing his identification with the monster, John comes face to face with his own death. Moreover, by recognising the productive potential of apparently female emotions, and drawing on the film's narrative origins in Du Maurier's short story, *Don't Look Now* functions in terms of Diana Wallace's 'uncanny stories', female Gothic stories which 'use the unexplained supernatural and … evade the marriage ending' in order to 'offer especially fertile and sophisticated explorations of women's dreams and desires, fears and terrors' (2004, p. 58; p. 66; original emphasis). *Don't Look Now* subverts those tropes of the Gothic in its critique of 1970s patriarchal culture.

Over and over, horror films of the 1970s 'contradict normal idealised family images', and subvert the symbolic association of the family with hope and futurity (Williams 1996, pp. 13-14), and depict an 'increasing thematic preoccupation with male insecurity' (Street 2009, pp. 93-94). Indeed, Tony Williams goes so far as to argue that 'all horror films are really family horror films containing psychic mechanisms that are derived from clinical cases associated with dysfunctional families', and that they represent 'a response to cultural discourses' (1996, p. 18; p. 26). Certainly, critics agree, since *Psycho*, *Rosemary's Baby* and *The Texas Chainsaw Massacre* horror has been 'implicitly recognised … as familial; that the threat posed by the monster to society, far from being an external one, is created by repression within the family' (Towlson 2014, p. 98; see also Roche 2014, pp. 65-66; pp. 84-85; Sobchack 1996, p. 143; and Worland 2007, p. 87). The patriarchal figure in such films is under threat, not only by alternative forms of knowledge (as in the psychic knowledge which contradicts John's certainties in *Don't Look Now*), but by the erasure of the child, the locus of the family's futurity and the law of primogeniture. For the way in which it signifies such threats to traditional cultural institutions, then, the family, is the site of 1970s horror. *Don't Look Now*, however, situates this as a failure of patriarchal emotional knowledge and a fundamental misreading of the locus of threat.

Street has lamented the fact that '[a]lthough *Don't Look Now* was a critical and box-office success ... it did not result in more quality horror projects which might have saved the genre from decline during [the 1970s]' (2009, p. 95). Her complaint is true enough, but in recognising the originality and cultural significance of Roeg's film, this study seeks to come closer to a recognition not only of the cultural function of the horror film, but of the representation of trauma in horror cinema more generally. In attending to the affective capacity of *Don't Look Now*, we can see the theoretical and social significance of trauma narratives in the 1970s.

FOOTNOTES

1. For a clear explanation of the differences between horror films of the 1930s-1940s and the 1960s-1970s, see Towlson 2014, pp. 104-105.
2. Rick Worland argues that *The Exorcist*, for example, makes reference to the Vietnam War, signalling 'the precise hot-button political anxieties underlying the movie's phenomenal reception. The climax, with the girl saved but the priests dead, resonantly suggested that the battle between good and evil as the film defined it had ended at best in an exhausting and uneasy draw' (2007, p. 100).

Chapter 1: Looking Again: The Critical Heritage

> Dear Mr Roeg, I watched your film of my story and your John and Laura reminded me so much of a young couple I saw in Torcello having lunch together. They looked so handsome and beautiful and yet they seemed to have a terrible problem and I watched them with sadness. The young man tried to cheer his wife up but to no avail and it struck me perhaps that their child had died of meningitis … (Du Maurier cited in Houtman 2009)

Don't Look Now is striking in its representation of the effects of trauma and anxiety on the grieving parent. Yet, existing studies of the film have not yet examined it, or the short story by Daphne Du Maurier from which it is adapted, in the context of contemporary trauma theory. Instead, the extant research privileges the narrative's Gothic and horror influences in more general terms, particularly through its representation of gender and sexuality (especially the concept of the 'monstrous feminine'), its thematic and symbolic interest in vision and blindness, primarily Jungian psychoanalysis of symbols and archetypes, the Venetian setting as a site of Otherness and alienation, and the innovative cinematic techniques Roeg employs in the construction of the film. The result is a privileging of symbolic discourses as they appear in the film, and an alignment of the narrative with Roeg's other films of the 1970s and early 1980s, rather than an understanding of *Don't Look Now* as emerging from and contributing to the discourse of 1970s cinematic horror, or its contextualisation within literary theory, including and especially trauma theory. This chapter contributes to an understanding of the film in the context of Du Maurier's Gothic narratives, with particular emphasis on those which had previously been adapted to film (especially *Rebecca* [1940] and *The Birds* [1963], both directed by Alfred Hitchcock, to whom Roeg pays homage early in *Don't Look Now*), and Roeg's earlier films, particularly those which deal with themes of trauma and violence (this includes both of the films Roeg directed prior to *Don't Look Now*, *Performance* [1970] and *Walkabout* [1971], as well as others on which he worked as cameraman: *Fahrenheit 451* [1966], and *Petulia* [1968], which cast Roeg's apparent 'muse', and one of the stars of *Don't Look Now*, Julie Christie). Developing my discussion of 1970s horror cinema in the introduction to this study, I propose that we read both Du Maurier and

Roeg's works within the context of mid- to late-twentieth-century British culture, considering them as particularly concerned to depict the cultural traumas of the period. Although there are some distinctive differences between the film and the story from which it is adapted, and the film should, of course, be analysed on its own terms, we must not forget that *Don't Look Now* is adapted from a literary text, and that this may have implications for the representations and adaptations of trauma in contemporary literature and film. The aim of this chapter is to review the existing studies of the film and the story from which it is adapted, with a particular eye to considering the way in which the present study might extend and augment those discussions by attending to the cinematic and narrative language of trauma offered up by *Don't Look Now*. It is not intended to dismiss those extant interpretations: far from it. Rather, this chapter interrogates *Don't Look Now*'s critical heritage as both avoiding and approaching the ever-retreating position of the trauma-text: a simultaneous recognition and avowal of the film's horror and its anxieties.

Roeg has never been considered a mainstream filmmaker; indeed, he does not fit the primary discourses of national cinema, his work being neither art house nor commercial, and he is even excluded from Robert Shail's study of British cinema in the 1970s for this reason (Patch 2010a, p. 255). Neil Sinyard even goes so far as to argue that the properties of Roeg's films are in opposition to those of British cinema more generally (1991, p. 2). *Don't Look Now*, however, differs in this respect. In one sense, it is precisely this site of difference which marks the distinctive horror of *Don't Look Now*, which was ultimately to be one of Roeg's most commercially successful films (Lanza 1989, p. 121). Certainly, it is, like his other films, a theoretically engaged work. In opposition to the conventional Hollywood popularism of *The Exorcist*, for example, *Don't Look Now* is situated within the context of 1970s critical theory, such as deconstruction and reader response theory (1989, p. 36).[3] In fact, it is this kind of textual openness, or engagement with the audience as a process of meaning-making, which for Roeg is a mark of a film's success. 'Roeg assaults conventions,' Joseph Lanza notes, 'because he strongly believes that warring interpretations, even those rubbing against the creator's intent, are a movie's barometer of success. He lets the public know that he prefers to see the world through a camera whose viewpoint is misaligned' (ibid.). Yet, in a move away from the highly aesthetic forms of his first two directed films, Roeg selected *Don't Look Now* as his next project because of its emphasis on story (Salwolke 1993, p. 37). He wanted, he noted in an interview, to film a 'yarn' (Milne and Houston 1973, p. 3). To be sure, *Don't Look Now* follows a clearer and more conventional narrative arc than did either *Performance* or *Walkabout*, but it is hardly a conventional narrative film in any other sense. Instead, it draws from the familiar tropes of perhaps one of the most conventional genres, the Gothic, to be found in both Du Maurier's story and other horror films of the 1960s and 1970s. Rather than simply 'learning the tropes' of this genre, as Sanderson argues (1996, p. 23), I show in this study that the viewer of *Don't Look Now* must combine them with the discourses of late twentieth-century critical theory in order to comment on the function of emotion, for both character and viewer, in contemporary horror narratives.

In this respect, it is also notable that Roeg selected a story by du Maurier for his 'yarn' film since, as Sanderson has observed, 'her insistence on sound and vision makes her an intensely cinematic writer' (1996, p. 14). Hitchcock adapted three of her works to film – *Jamaica Inn* (1939), *Rebecca* and *The Birds* – and Roeg was certainly influenced by those adaptations, as well as Hitchcock's other works: the cut from Laura's scream in the opening scene to the sound of a hammer drill in Venice is a much commented upon technique drawn from Hitchcock's *The 39 Steps* (1935). The scream might echo, too, Janet Leigh's scream in the infamous shower scene of *Psycho*, and which might be said to herald the coming decades of interest in horror cinema. It is perhaps *Rebecca*, however, which might be traced as the most prominent influence on Roeg's adaptation. Like *Don't Look Now*, it is a narrative marked by anxiety: the young, unnamed, second wife of Maxim de Winter comes to Manderley, his large waterside property, to find it haunted by reminders of his first wife, Rebecca. Both film and novel emphasise the narrator's limited perspective, as she struggles to negotiate Rebecca's ghostly presence and the imposing home of which she is now mistress. Indeed, each shot works to diminish the second Mrs de Winter in contrast to the overwhelming size of Manderley and the constant surveillance of its housekeeper, Mrs Danvers. If *Rebecca* is quintessentially Gothic in its depiction of the haunted house, the ambiguous husband (echoes of *Bluebeard*), and the ghosts of the past, *Don't Look Now* troubles the extent to which those tropes can be used to read and understand contemporary horror. The house haunted by the death of the child has been left behind, and is replaced by a city tormented by the expectation of murder; the husband who questions his wife's sanity for her belief in psychic contact with their lost child is the one chased through the labyrinthine streets; and the ghosts of history are explicitly returned to the present, rather than repressed or denied, in John's project of restoration. Ultimately what is at stake here is the extent to which du Maurier's 'good old-fashioned yarn' works as a model for Roeg's cinema narrative since, like John, at every turn our expectations of the familiar satisfactions of story are thwarted.

Figure 1: The original poster advertisement for *Don't Look Now.* (Source: IMDB)

From its earliest reviews, the film received a mixed reception, not only in terms of its popularity but more particularly in its viewers' recognition of the film's affective work. Jay Cocks (1973) recognised its 'continual, mounting anxiety', and emphasised the film's psychoanalytic influences, comparing it to the psychological terror of Henry James's novella, *The Turn of the Screw* (1898), rather than to the corporeal horror of *The Exorcist*. Vincent Canby (1973), too, compared the film to *The Turn of the Screw*, but not favourably, and argued that the film fails in its construction of suspense; indeed, he noted that the powerful love-making scene is essentially 'comic', and sees Roeg's use of prolepsis as simply a 'device'. The promotional poster may have in some way contributed to these conflicting interpretations: billing *Don't Look Now* as 'a psychic thriller', the poster features a concerned-looking Christie and Sutherland as a photograph in an ornate Gothic frame, from which blood mysteriously pours. The tag line, 'Pass the warning', bears little connection to the image; and the image, indeed, bears little relation to the film. The frame calls up the family photographs which adorn the mantelpiece of the sisters' hotel room, suggesting, perhaps, that they saw the Baxters' fate even before they had met them. The blood seeping from the photograph echoes, of course, the bleeding slide which provokes John's first experience of precognition. As a whole, then, the poster suggests an inevitable trauma which will befall the Baxters and their family; to 'pass the warning', however, is to focus the narrative on the sisters and their determination to influence the Baxters' course of action, rather than on the Baxters themselves and their failure to recognise the trauma into which they rush headlong. It is in this sense, perhaps, that the film's affective and Gothic discourses become confused.

Sanderson's is, to date, the only extant book-length study of the film. As part of the British Film Institute's Modern Classics series, it focuses on the film's position in cinema history, the historical and personal context for the actors and director in making the film, and on brief analyses of some of the film's key scenes. In particular, it includes shot-by-shot analyses of the opening and closing sequences. Although Sanderson does argue for the film's construction of strangeness and alienation in the Venetian context, as well as for the black comedy of the final scene, it is primarily contextual and descriptive in its concerns, and bears little engagement with the film's critical background. That critical heritage has, unsurprisingly, given its label as a 'psychic thriller', been heavily influenced by Freudian and Jungian psychoanalysis. Chuck Kleinhans (1974), in one of the earliest critical readings of the film, makes this point about Roeg's *oeuvre* in general, noting that they 'lend themselves to Freudian interpretation easily', since Roeg 'is fascinated with the basic oral fantasy of engulfment, of losing the boundaries of oneself'. His point is a valuable one, even if it does fail to recognise the numerous other ways in which Freudian psychoanalysis appears to influence films like *Don't Look Now*, such as its engagement with trauma. George Toles, for example, in a critical interpretation which perhaps comes the closest to the present study, reads the threat of failing to see 'in time' through the film's use of repetition; in this sense, he argues, '[s]eeing is hauntingly and ironically belated; none of the countless ephemeral *nows* that John tries to absorb and that make up his narrative existence can take him off his preordained path or alert him to the true crisis that shapes his end (an end, in fact, already shaped)' (2013, p. 119; original emphasis). That failure to recognise or to see is also central to Gina Wisker's reading of Du Maurier's story, which takes, as its stimulus, Du Maurier's observation in a 1957 letter that '[t]he evil in us comes to the surface. Unless we recognise it in time, accept it, understand it, we are all destroyed, just as the people in *The Birds* were destroyed' (cited in Wisker 1999, p. 19), in order to show how her story 'is a version of horror which builds on the Gothic as critique and subversion of the conventional and the taken for granted' (1999, p. 23). Both Toles and Wisker observe the intersection of horror and humour in *Don't Look Now*, but for Roeg, 'the Gothic is a tremendous cultural influence, not a funny thing at all' (cited in Milne and Houston 1973, p. 7). The Gothic as it appears in *Don't Look Now* is instead best understood in terms of its relation to psychoanalysis, to the ways in which we are haunted by our own minds.

Jungian readings of the film have drawn on the function of archetypes and symbols, as in James Palmer and Michael Riley's study, in which patterns of symbolism come to show what they call the film's 'own clairvoyance' (1995, p. 22). John Izod asserts that fate and ancient myths appear in all of Roeg's films, and adopts Carl Jung's theories throughout his book-length study of Roeg's work. Indeed, he argues, *Don't Look Now*, for both character and viewer, 'can be described as a search for the meaning of an image' and, too, to recover the symbolic and clairvoyant power of the psyche (1992, p. 67; p. 79). Myth is also the focus of Marsha Kinder and Beverle Houston's study (1978), although rather than the work of Jung they draw on myth as it appears in the theories of Claude Lévi-Strauss.

It is symbolism, however, which is the most dominant means of reading *Don't Look Now*, and which has featured most prominently in the critical heritage since Cocks's (1973) claim that the film's images always and everywhere work together in a structure of meaning, so that '[e]very shot and image is like a tile in the mosaic of the church under restoration'. Although Michael Dempsey's review of *Don't Look Now* finds its symbolism and coincidences contrived (1974, p. 39), later critics have observed the way in which the profusion of apparently important images mean that, as Joseph Gomez has it, 'the viewer is hard pressed to distinguish trivialities from profound shots which do, indeed, reveal significant visual motifs essential to the structure of the film' (1981, p. 49).[4] Tom Milne made a similar point in his early review, suggesting '[d]on't look now, Roeg might be saying, but every time you hear or see something, your mind is drawing connections and conclusions from depths of which you know nothing' (1973, p. 237). Indeed, Roeg himself has stated that image, for him, is what is critical to the creation of film narrative, observing: 'I create images and tell stories on film ... and if you're dealing with *thought* on film, then I think it's cheating to use literary means. I want people to read the *images* in my films' (cited in Kennedy 1980; original emphases). For Andrew Patch and, too, for Elizabeth Watkins, that symbolism – most powerfully, the colour red – is primarily a function of colour, showing 'an evolving network of connections' in the narrative (Patch 2010b, p. 72; Watkins 2015, p. 436). Desmond O'Rawe also draws on the significance of the colour red, but emphasises the way in which the dwarf's red coat comes to stand out against the wintry, mythical background of Venice as setting (2005, p. 224; p. 227). Finally, Sue Harper and Justin Smith make the connection between colour, symbol and psychoanalysis, and conclude that John's psychic abilities are expressed as patterns, and that '[t]hese pattern-recognitions function throughout the film as a sort of prolepsis of his awful end' (2012b, p. 165).

Less frequent are interpretations of *Don't Look Now* in terms of its cultural, social or cinematic context. Jim Leach has, however, recognised Roeg's 'formal and sexual "daring"' in the context of 1960s and 1970s cinema (2006, p. 195), while Kinder and Houston compare *Don't Look Now* to its precursors, *The Exorcist* and *Rosemary's Baby*, particularly in terms of their treatment of the supernatural, suggesting that Roeg's 'radical chic of the late 1960s and early 1970s' works alongside a recognition of the importance of culture, tradition and the past in order to understand and create the future (1987, p. 45; p. 52). More often, such sociocultural readings consider the significance of gender in *Don't Look Now*, particularly as it pertains to gendered forms of knowledge; that is, the masculine/rational versus the feminine/supernatural. Thus Coral Houtman (2009) argues that in both film and story, *Don't Look Now* 'dramatises sexual difference as a dangerous division, pervasive both within nature and within the psyche, inherent in both men and women', while Mark Gallagher observes Roeg's tendency in all of his work to both reproduce and critique 'normative masculinity' as a challenge 'to dominant worldviews' (2004, pp. 162-63), and Kristi Wilson sees John as a 'white male professional' under threat by unknown and unacknowledged emotional (read: feminine) forces (1999, p. 284).

While, therefore, there has been continuing critical interest in *Don't Look Now* since its release in the early 1970s, these critical concerns have clustered around a few key concepts. Although the present study does make use of many of these perspectives, it ultimately attempts to read both this film and late twentieth-century horror cinema more generally in terms of its affective structures and its contribution to the critical theory of trauma. By addressing *Don't Look Now* in terms of the ways in which it recasts the 1970s horror film precisely as a narrative of trauma and anxiety, this study seeks not only to provide an innovative approach to this film, but also to suggest more generally the critical relationships between the horror film and affect theory and their use for our understanding of the cultural ethics of narrative. This book therefore recognises *Don't Look Now* as a narrative in which the two converge, provoking a critical re-evaluation of the psychoanalysis of cinematic fear.

FOOTNOTES

3. Robert Phillip Kolker's 'The Open Texts of Nicolas Roeg' (1977) is evidence of this trend.
4. Dempsey is also critical of Du Maurier's original story, calling it 'romantic sludge' (1974, p. 39).

Chapter 2: Dread and the Trauma of Complicity

When John meets with the police inspector following the report that his wife is missing, the officer asks him: 'What is it you fear?' 'A killer on the loose; a murderer,' John responds, but with some doubt in his voice. In some sense, this is true: John has already witnessed the body of a victim being unceremoniously pulled from the murky canal water, and heard a terrible scream while lost in the Venice streets at night. Yet, what John appears to fear, paradoxically both more specifically and in a way even more vague, is the death or loss of his wife, another woman for whom he feels responsible and whom he has apparently failed to protect. His fear, then, is that yet again, he has failed to see or know in time, failed to recognise the trauma before it has occurred. In earlier chapters of this book, I have made the case that *Don't Look Now* offers up an alternative kind of horror to those most common in 1970s Britain and America. Specifically, it is a film concerned with the horror of parental anxiety – the terrible knowledge that one has failed to prepare for danger and to protect the child. In this chapter, I consider the film's suspense, its sense of threat or danger, in this context. Drawing on Sigmund Freud's conceptualisation of anxiety (or *angstbereitschaft*) as 'dreading forward', I argue that rather than being a narrative of traumatic repetition and compulsion, *Don't Look Now* is driven by John's desire to paradoxically prevent his daughter's death after it has occurred, and thereby to overcome his sense of complicity in her drowning. Unlike in Du Maurier's story, in which Christine dies of meningitis, John and Laura are unable to prepare, even briefly, for their child's death. Indeed, we, and they, never see the accident itself. John's 'psychic' abilities, therefore, are best understood as 'dreading forward', or what I have elsewhere called 'traumatic clairvoyance' (Gildersleeve 2014, p. 56) – they depict his confused experience of trauma (the horror of his own death) prior to its occurrence, and as a result of the past trauma (the horror of Christine's death). In this way, although John hopes that he will fulfil his patriarchal responsibilities, in time, this time, his authority is undermined by his failure to recognise knowledge of a different (perhaps more feminine) kind.

Clairvoyance, premonitions, telekinesis and other forms of psychic abilities were popular tropes in 1970s horror cinema. John Kenneth Muir explains the phenomenon as a turn away from hard science, arguing that 'because science had proven so lousy at handling many of America's problems, audiences turned to more "extreme" possibilities in the 1970s, hence the resurgence of films about psychic powers' (2002, p. 32). Muir's justification would align 1970s horror with a similar resurgence of interest in psychic mediums and spectral engagement in the years during and following the First World War, in which a home front audience, desperate for news of lost loved ones, saw a rise in activities like séances, spirit photography and psychic performances. Equally, however, we might see this revived interest in the psychic as a return to the post-psychoanalysis Gothic narratives of the late nineteenth and early twentieth centuries. In the work of Poe and Charlotte Perkins Gilman, for example, what is to be feared is not the foreign, monstrous Other, but the unknown Self. In this sense, *Don't Look Now* might be seen to mark a return to more traditional psychoanalytic fears about the self and the experience of traumatic events. To be sure, the film was followed in that decade by several other films with similar preoccupations. *Carrie*, *Ruby* (dir. Curtis Harrington, 1977), *Jennifer* (dir. Brice Mack, 1978), *Patrick* (dir. Richard Franklin, 1978), *Tourist Trap* (dir. David Schmoeller, 1978) and *The Fury* (dir. Brian De Palma, 1978) all depict characters who kill using their psychic or telekinetic powers (Muir 2002, pp. 32-33). By the same token, in *Deep Red* (dir. Dario Argento, 1975) and *Eyes of Laura Mars* (dir. Irvin Kershner, 1978), psychic characters are able to read the minds of murderers, anticipating their next attacks, and in *The Shining*, the child's psychic abilities mean that he is able to save himself and his mother from his crazed/possessed father. Where *Don't Look Now* differs from these other films of its decade, however, is in its ambiguity about the validity of such powers. John and Laura conflict with one another not only in their responses to their daughter's death, but in their beliefs in the sisters' claims to have seen Christine's spirit with the couple in Venice. While other 1970s films dealing with psychic abilities do not question their verisimilitude, part of the horror of *Don't Look Now* resides in its magic realism: the horror of the possibility of the unknown, of the way in which this can encroach on the apparently secure borders of the Enlightenment self. Moreover, the film does not resolve this tension: John's premonitions might just as easily be hallucinations; his reading of symbols a sign of his desperation to form a coherent narrative in the wake of trauma. In this sense, *Don't Look Now*'s interest in the psychic is perhaps best understood not in its most literal sense, but as a form of anxiety or dread, of traumatic clairvoyance.

In a 1985 interview, Roeg insisted that his task in *Don't Look Now*, 'like anyone who works in any form of art, is to express an emotion' (cited in Salwolke 1993, p. ix). That emotion, I argue here, is anxiety. Other critics of *Don't Look Now* commonly describe its circularity and recurring motifs in terms of a Freudian repetition compulsion and the processes of unresolved mourning. That is, rather than adopting the 'healthy' process of narrativisation and working through, John and Laura are suggested to be stuck in the melancholic denial of their daughter's death and an inability to move forward from it. Lisa Downing, for example, argues that 'the symbolism of water ... will be deployed throughout the film to suggest the eternal return, the compulsion to repeat the association between birth and death', noting that 'it is to stagnant water that the mourning couple are drawn' (2011, pp. 52-53). In other words, their very insistence on visiting Venice, the city of canals, stages a repetition of their home, and the stagnant pool of water beside it, which they failed to recognise as a threat until it was too late. Ironically, of course, they again fail to recognise the threat which is in front of them; John, in particular, might be said to simply replay the past as he attempts to rescue the figure which plays dangerously by the water, while Laura rushes back to England to care for their other child, who is injured at school – although once again the child has been abandoned and required to fend for himself. Richard Armstrong, perhaps more interestingly, has shown how *Don't Look Now* 'positioned itself within a psychological affect-driven historical continuum ... one of the most explicit forerunners of modern mourning cinema' (2012, p. 82). It is, he says, 'crucially a film about the inevitability of death', as well as 'its consequences for those who survive' (2012, p. 88). Rather than considering the dread of that inevitability as the film's affective discourse, however, Armstrong returns to the logic of mourning. Since John, he suggests, never speaks of Christine because he cannot 'describe how he feels', he may be said to suffer from melancholic incorporation (2012, p. 89). However, Sandor Ferenczi's incorporation constitutes a denial of the love object's absence; by incorporating the loved one into the psyche, the subject keeps the love object alive and does not have to confront the loss. John's behaviour in this respect does not align with the project of incorporation. True, he chases the red-cloaked figure through the streets, attempting to cajole and save her. In one sense, this might be read as repetition: the desire to save this 'child' as he was not able to do for his own. It is not, however, an example of incorporation: John is entirely aware that this figure is not Christine. 'I'm coming,' he says; 'I'm a friend. I won't hurt you.' His attention is caught by the similarity, but he does not suffer from the delusion that his daughter has been resurrected, or that she is, in a way, haunting her parents. Indeed, he insists to Laura that their child is 'dead, dead, dead!' *Don't Look Now* is best understood, then, as engaging with the affective discourse of anxiety, rather than a project of mourning or melancholia.

Freud describes anxiety, or *Angstbereitschaft* (anxiety-preparedness) in *Inhibitions, Symptoms and Anxiety* (1926) as a state of activity in preparation for the passivity of an anticipated 'danger-situation':

> When the individual becomes able to foresee a danger-situation and to prepare for it, instead of waiting passively until it arrives, this denotes an important advance in the capacity for self-protection. In this situation of expectation – the danger-situation – the ego can send out a 'signal of anxiety'. (Quinodoz 2005, p. 223)

Anxiety is therefore *opposed* to the process of traumatic repetition: rather than unconsciously repeating the trauma of the past, the anxious subject is vigilant precisely against doing so. The traumatic event is not forgotten or repressed, as is the case for the melancholic; rather, the anxious subject remembers the event and their original failure to prepare, and desires to prevent its recurrence, and thus the recurrence of trauma, in the future. In Freud's terms, then, if 'the present situation reminds me of one of the traumatic experiences I have had before ... I will anticipate the trauma and behave as though it had already come, while there is yet time to turn aside' (1936, p. 161). Anxiety, then, is the practice of 'dreading forward', as Lyndsey Stonebridge puts it – the experience of expected fear, the anticipation of traumatic return, before it can happen again (2011, p. 6).

Don't Look Now's horror, therefore, does not, or does not primarily, derive from 'surprise', as Lawrence Shaffer has it, but rather from expectation (1974, p. 8). Sanderson has perhaps come closest to this identification of anxiety as it appears in *Don't Look Now* when he argues that the film's 'paranoia' is 'infectious' (1996, p. 30). Certainly, anxiety possesses attributes of paranoia in its obsessive anticipation of the traumatic future expected to come. It is also true that this paranoia may be said to spread to the film's audience as, like John, we come to obsessively (mis)read the false signs of traumatic return. However, the film's paranoia does not function in isolation; rather, it is always already a function of its anxiety. Any 'infection' which takes place, therefore, is of anxiety as much as it is of paranoia. Like John, the audience dreads the repetition of trauma, and similarly reads signs of its return. I take up this concept of traumatic misreading in further detail in Chapter Three. In this chapter, however, I want to consider *Don't Look Now*'s anxiety in terms of the loss of a child.

The 1960s and 1970s were not only a period in which cinema became preoccupied with the terror of psychic precognition. This was also the time in which the figure of the child emerged as a site of terror. *The Omen*, *Rosemary's Baby*, and later, *Children of the Corn* (a story written by Stephen King in 1977, adapted to film in 1984 [dir. Fritz Kiersch]), all associate the child with satanic or demonic power and the destruction of an adult community. *Carrie* and *The Shining*, also original 1970s narratives by King adapted to film in the late 1970s and early 1980s, on the other hand, figure the child or adolescent as possessing supernatural powers which can be used for good or evil. Indeed, as Vivian Sobchack has shown, as 'horror film children grow smaller, younger, and less adolescent, their special powers slowly diminish from apocalyptic fury to a relatively helpless insight' (1996, p. 152). *Don't Look Now* differs from these other films, of course, in that Christine is neither possessed by demonic spirits nor possessed of supernatural powers. Rather, the horror associated with Christine derives from what her death implies about her family, and specifically about the failures of her parents and the domestic space of the late twentieth century. For Sobchack, from around the late 1960s, the figure of the child came to signify something larger – 'a contemporary and pressing cultural drama':

> That drama emerges from the crisis experienced by American bourgeois patriarchy since the late 1960s and is marked by the related disintegration and transfiguration of the traditional American bourgeois family – an ideological as well as interpersonal structure characterised ... by its cellular construction and institutionalisation of capitalist and patriarchal relations and values (among them, monogamy, heterosexuality, and consumerism) and by its present state of disequilibrium and crisis. (1996, p. 144)

In other words, the destabilised or threatening child is a sign of the destabilised and threatened patriarch. This also applies to the patriarchal home, the physical site of his dominion. In earlier Gothic texts, the apparent protection of the home can be seen to produce 'anxiety', Cavallaro argues, since its security simultaneously 'assert[s] the outside world's irreducible alterity' (2002, p. 147). However, as the patriarch's grip is loosened and the security of the family is shown to be a myth in contemporary horror films, so too does that Other find its way in. 'A man's home in bourgeois patriarchal culture', as Sobchack puts it, 'is no longer his castle'; his reign over the family is undermined as the boundaries between the self (or family) and private space, and the foreign Other and public space, are dissolved (1996, pp. 145-47). In the late 1970s, in particular, 'the genre begins to overtly interrogate paternal commitment and its relation to patriarchal power', so that 'as patriarchy is challenged ... the horror film plays out the rage of paternal responsibility denied the economic and political benefits of patriarchal power' (1996, p. 152).

The family – and more precisely its disruption – is central to many horror films of the decade. *Halloween* and *A Nightmare on Elm Street* (1984), for example, both feature broken families and abandoned children; in each case, the killer preys on those made vulnerable by such breaks between parents and children. The result is that it is parents, not only the villain, who are made monstrous; the father in particular is subject to this critique, since it is he who has failed in his authority. What this means, then, is an equation in which the relative power of the child or the father constitutes a threat to the other (1996, p. 156). This takes on a particular significance in *Don't Look Now* given that Christine's death does not appear to be felt as the loss of the child as such, but as a failure of parenthood. Margarida Morgado, for example, has suggested that films like *Don't Look Now* are 'significant for our panic-stricken, anxious times regarding the safety of children', but more particularly adds that

> One of the striking features of these texts lies in the fact that parents claim the absence of children for themselves. The disappearance of children, daughters, is the starting point for gripping narratives of parental grief, emphasising the hurting void left by children in the family, the purposelessness of adult lives without children, and the disintegration of societies unable to care for and protect the lives and well-being of their children. (2002, p. 248)

The horror of *Don't Look Now*, then, is not the horror of the lost child, but the horror of failed parenthood – Christine is what Lisa Downing calls 'a cipher for [her] parents' – and for heteronormative culture's – threatened values and hopes' (2011, p. 61). This not only explains John's desire to save what he imagines to be the child lost along the canals of Venice, but also the Baxters' decision to send Johnny to boarding school immediately following Christine's death: this is not a repetition compulsion but a sign that their own ability to care for their children is felt to be so at risk that they entrust his care to professionals. Their anxiety is allayed, in other words, by removing themselves from proximity to the remaining child, and is stoked by reminders of their responsibilities, as when the psychic sisters tell them that Christine is still with them, or when Johnny's headmaster telephones to advise the Baxters of his injury at school. Downing argues that John's pursuit of the 'child' figure constitutes a kind of suicide, 'a dereliction of the duty owed to life-drive and to reproductive futurism', since as a 'failed father' he has 'no capacity for furthering futurity' (2011, p. 54). Anxiety, however, is directly opposed to this kind of drive, what we might describe as the death-drive. Anxiety anticipates destruction and works precisely against its occurrence. What we might see, then, is that when Johnny is injured, Laura's anxiety is triggered and she must rush to care for him; John's anxiety, too, is instigated by the incident, and it is only once this has happened that he becomes obsessed by the red-coated figure and by the care of his wife. His pursuit is not the pursuit of death, an attempt to atone for or perhaps align with his failures, then, but a figure of the desire to prevent it.

The film features three key scenes which are invested with this desire to see and to know in time, to be prepared, to overcome death: the opening scene, in which Christine dies; the love-making scene, in which John and Laura are reunited; and the funeral barge scene, in which John is convinced he sees Laura in Venice when he had thought she was on her way to England. Each of these scenes is marked by its temporal collapse and the coalescing of present and future (Salwolke 1993, p. 38). They do not only work to signify John's precognitive abilities, however, but to exemplify the processes of anxiety at work in the film.

The opening scene of *Don't Look Now* is one of the most-discussed aspects of the film. Scott Salwolke, for example, argues that it 'is among the most haunting scenes in cinema. The scene does not only contain John's futile effort to save [Christine], it also intimates his own fate' (1993, p. 39). What has not been recognised, however, is the way in which it functions to anticipate John and Laura's later behaviour, as they anxiously seek to prevent the repetition of the trauma. The film's opening two opening shots are, first, of rain falling on a pond; second, of a blinded window, as rays of sunlight stream through the gaps. John's soft humming can be heard in the background. It is only later that the second image can be interpreted: it is the window of the Baxters' hotel room in Venice, and it also foreshadows the gates which John closes behind himself and his murderer as he gives chase. The shot is significant, Sinyard argues, not only because it shows the 'present and the future operating side by side', making us retrospectively uncertain of our temporal position (1991, p. 44). In addition, he notes, 'because of editing which forges a link between unlikely material and forces these uncanny correspondences on our attention, [we] are endowed with second sight and our scepticism about extrasensory perception is broken down by filmic means' (ibid.). While Sinyard's interpretation holds true with respect to a reading of the film which emphasises its interest in John's latent psychic abilities, it is also the case that this shot, and the little-discussed shot of the pond which precedes it, establishes the film's affective discourse of anxiety. That is, while several critics have noted the significance of the window, it has not been viewed in conjunction with the shot of the pond. The intercut images not only confuse past and present: they establish the way in which past and present are confused for John and Laura, as they both remember and anticipate the traumatic event, both in the moment and after it. The pond, marked by rain, always already precedes any memory of the event in which it also features. The Baxters are, in other words, always already anticipating, in the moment of, and recalling the moment of, trauma.

The point is underscored by later parts of the scene. It presents an idyllic pastoral vision: John and Laura chat inside by the fire, working and reading on a chilly afternoon. Their children, Johnny and Christine, play separately outside, although Johnny keeps an occasional eye on his younger sister. A white horse gallops across the field – a symbol, Lanza has argued, for innocence (1989, p. 46) – while Christine pushes a small wheelbarrow across the grass. The scene is laden with nostalgia for a simpler, happier time: its rural vision of English family life figures a sharp contrast to the urban, European lifestyle the Baxters inhabit after Christine's death. Although the child often came to represent a threatening figure in horror cinema of the 1970s, Christine seems to

Figure 2: Laura and a bystander attempt to reach John through the locked gates at the film's conclusion.

hearken back to an older symbolisation of the child as associated with innocence or nostalgia: '[w]hat seems a looking forward toward the possibilities of the future is a longing backward toward the promise once possessed by the past – a longing for inexperience, for potential rather than realised action, for an openness to the world based on a lack of worldliness' (Sobchack 1996, p. 149).

Figure 3: Christine pushes a wheelbarrow in the garden while a horse gallops in the background.

However, it is also the case that Christine plays with a soldier doll – an unlikely toy, perhaps, for the nostalgia of rural girlhood, especially given that while the doll is dressed as a soldier in a gas-mask on its upper half, its lower half is costumed in a skirt; it also speaks in a female voice as Christine pulls the string in its back, throws the ball into the pond, and creeps toward it clutching the doll close to her chest. As she crouches towards the ball, balancing precariously on a narrow bridge, the camera pans to the reflection of her back in the dark water. The sequence suggests not simply, then, a nostalgia for rural innocence (as Christine plays with the wheelbarrow), but more specifically for the way in which this has been corrupted by the trauma of urbanisation, technology, war, and even changes in gender roles. In some ways, Christine's play suggests, her death has been caused by the failure to anticipate her daring and mimicry, and to prepare her to protect herself as she engages in this type of play. That Christine has also asked her mother a difficult question ('If the earth is round, why is a frozen pond flat?') underscores this point: this girl-child is not content to accept the world around her, but interrogates it. It is the failure to prepare her for the consequences of those interrogations, to anticipate the trauma which may follow, which leads to her death. Her brother, too, rides his bike (rather than the horse), and must find a puncture in the wheel (he is cut by a shard of glass stuck in the tyre) after he rides over and shatters a stray pane of glass hidden in the grass. Roeg has commented on the glass as symbol, too, noting that it

> … stemmed from a story, a personal story. A friend of mine might have been able to save … to prevent a dreadful incident … he said … *if* he'd been able to break some glass at the time. Apart from any symbolic quality, glass sets up a sensation of fear, of something dangerous and brittle. This is built into everyone. Almost everyone has a fear of shattered glass. Mirrors and glass, glass especially, so fragile … so firm at one moment and so dangerous the next, it's frightening. (Cited in Milne and Houston 1973, p. 4; original emphasis)

What we might also recognise, however, is the way in which the glass suggests the lurking or latent nature of trauma, so that even in the apparent idyll of the family's afternoon, rupture is lying in wait.[5]

Christine's dangerous running along the muddy banks of the pond also makes this clear, signifying not only what is immediately to come (the trauma of her death) but also John's later misrecognition of the hooded figure as it similarly runs and leaps by the canals. That Christine's movement is depicted as a reflection in the pond, showing her to run upside down, or in reverse (as if on a photographic slide of the kind her father uses), suggests that, as John has it, '[n]othing is what it seems'. Anxious about her fate, the film (or her parents' memories) attempts to rewind Christine's actions, to prevent the trauma before it occurs. The hurried series of shots which follows this – Christine steps into the shallow pond, while the sound of shattering glass echoes in the background; Laura flutters her fingers in front of her mouth while Christine covers her own mouth in a similar way; Johnny looks at the blood on his finger; John spills water on his slides, causing the red ink to run, like blood; Christine's ball falls into the pond – work to suggest the way in which the trauma becomes unpreventable. Just as Christine already favours her mother, so too her fate (the spilling of blood) has already been drawn.

Always and everywhere, then, the opening scene works to juxtapose past, present and future. As I have noted, however, this is not solely a means of demonstrating John's precognition, but to emphasise the processes of anxiety at work in the film – the ways in which future trauma is anticipated in the present moment. More than this, however, this anxious discourse works as part of John's construction of paternal guilt and his perception of his complicity in her death. If he had known sooner, if he had anticipated the trauma, the logic goes, then Christine's death would not have occurred. Indeed, the scene of Christine's death does not appear in the Du Maurier story (instead, it begins with the couple's dinner in Venice); this alteration, Sinyard argues, makes Christine's death seem 'in some way more the husband's fault' (1991, p. 42). This opening scene is imbued with the symbols of foresight John wishes he could have read. That he is voiceless as he emerges from the pond clutching Christine's limp body, his mouth shaped in a permanent 'O' of horror, suggests his regression to a pre-verbal state in which he ironically sees and knows more than he does in his intellectual work. The extradiegetic music as he stumbles from the water signifies a dream sequence – not a repetition compulsion in which he attempts to save his child, but an anxious return in which he permanently realises his paternal failure.

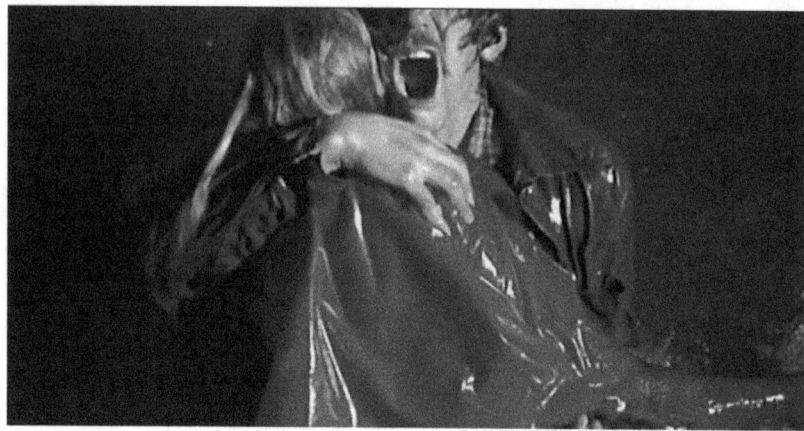

Figure 4: John clutches Christine's lifeless body in horror.

The love-making scene works in a similar fashion to the opening scene in its investment of the present with the knowledge of the future. The Baxters' first intimate reunion after Christine's death is intercut with shots of their post-coital preparation for dinner. The effect is a melancholic one, to be sure: it is to be the last evening they spend together in this way, and the proleptic shots work to suggest that it is over before it has even begun. That they emerge into the closed-up lobby of their hotel emphasises this point – the season is over, they are no longer welcome. Whereas the opening scene suggests the horror of realising one's failure to prepare, however, this scene suggests the blissful delusion of the couple's hope for the future. Indeed, it might be seen to be the only scene in the film that is free of anxiety: while the future is anticipated, it is not something for which one must prepare. Happiness here is in the moment of their connection and in the later memory of it.

Finally, the scene in which John believes he sees Laura and the psychic sisters on a funeral barge also makes use of the logic of anxiety. Like the love-making scene, it contains an anticipation or premonition of the future. Whereas the earlier scene's intercut shots code these temporal shifts as a remembering to come, however, in this scene the premonition is not explained as such until the film's conclusion. John's response to seeing the barge is confusion and panic: he assumes Laura has been kidnapped by the sisters, and immediately reports her disappearance to the police.

Figure 5: Laura and the sisters on the funeral barge.

This reaction is an anxious one: having lost Christine because of his failure to recognise the signs of her endangerment, he tries to prevent the recurrence of this loss by attempting to rescue his wife. The scene immediately follows one in which a dead body is pulled from the canal; while John watches on, a brief flashback notes the similarity of this drowned body to that of his daughter. It also occurs, of course, in the context of his son's injury at school, the reason for Laura's sudden departure from Venice. In Laura's absence, John is unable to monitor her safety. His separation from wife and son reminds him of his helplessness, a passivity underscored by his physical separation from her and the impossibility of giving chase as their barges pass in opposite directions. While John does not recognise his vision precisely as the future, then, he does respond in a way which mimics the anticipation of a future trauma and thus his anxious response to events which recall Christine's death.

While John's anxiety is more prevalent throughout the film, *Don't Look Now* does also establish Laura's behaviour within the logic of an anxious discourse. Whereas John works to prepare in time, this time, however, Laura's failure to do so may be seen to result in the family's second loss: John's death. The opening scene establishes Laura's shock (an absolute failure to prepare) in contrast to John's anticipation of the trauma. As he struggles wordlessly towards the house carrying Christine in his arms, Laura's fright, and the scream which links the scene to their future in Venice, is contrasted with his horrific awareness. Laura 'stumbles into knowing …. Caught entirely off-guard, she might be said to take in too much at once, in a single jolt' (Toles 2013, p. 112). Their contrasted reactions are also emphasised by the tempo of this scene, as Sinyard points out: while John's attempt to rescue his daughter is shown in slow motion, so that 'his grief seems excruciatingly prolonged', Laura's reaction is only shown after a 'calculated delay … with a number of cut-backs to her that increase the sense of anxiety and the impact when she does learn. When she sees, she sees *instantly*: it is an important contrast to her husband, who senses in advance, but reacts slowly to his intuitions and finally sees too late' (1991, p. 47). Laura's response to her parental failure is a symbolic return to the innocence and irresponsibility of childhood. Armstrong recognises this in the way in which Laura is repeatedly held between the two sisters, just as they say Christine sits between her parents and, too, in Laura and John's relationship, suggesting that in his indulgence and admonishment of her behaviours, and even his doling out of 'pocket money', 'they seem more like father and daughter than husband and wife' (2012, pp. 94-95). The scene in which, after her fainting spell, Laura waits in a hospital room for her husband, puts this behaviour into context. 'There's nothing but children out there', she exclaims to John – indeed, she has been taken to a children's hospital because it was the closest to the restaurant where she collapsed. She confesses to John that she fainted from the shock of hearing that Christine is 'still with us', but that now she 'feel[s] really great'. Her reassurance and recovery is not simply a function of the idea that Christine is, in spirit, still with her parents, but more specifically that she is still under their care. Just as the children with whom Laura plays in the hospital are kept protected behind a glass screen and a curtain, cared for in a safe room, so too now Christine, in death, can never again come to harm.[6] The children in the hospital play with a ball just like Christine's, but this ball will not bring them to harm, as it did her. They are always under surveillance, and though apparently ill or injured, do not appear to be so: they live in a bubble of happiness and play. After the Baxters leave the hospital, Laura insists that they stop at a church so that she can light a candle and pray for their daughter. Her act is a repetition of the protection of the children in hospital – a symbolic protection of Christine's spirit. Now, Laura need never again worry about her daughter and the anxiety-preparedness she failed to indulge at the film's beginning is repeated and justified. Her complicity in Christine's death is absolved.

Both John and Laura's reactions to the death of their daughter constitute anxiety, rather than the more commonly attributed mourning or melancholia following trauma. While both parents recognise their failure to know in time and thus to save Christine, their responses do differ. Laura finds a delusion of security in her faith that Christine's spirit still accompanies them. Paradoxically protected, now, by her death, Laura is absolved of any need to feel anxious about her safety or complicit in her continued absence. John, on the other hand, is preoccupied by his paternal failure. In both his memories of the past and his visions of the future, he not only attempts to prevent a recurrence of the trauma, but also relives the moment of his apparent guilt. *Don't Look Now* thus constructs a discourse of parental anxiety in response to trauma, a horror logic which persistently taunts the Baxters with their failures in both past and future.

FOOTNOTES

5. 'The sound of breaking glass which so ominously heralds the drowning … and later recurs equally shatteringly as glass is broken at two other moments of disaster, remains an association of crisis rather than a symbol or even a portent' (Milne 1973, p. 238).
6. For Houtman, the glass barrier 'emphasis[es] the inseparable barrier between Laura and her daughter, and perhaps also by association a glass barrier between Laura and John' (2009).

Chapter 3: *Destinerrance* and the Trauma of Misreading

> I wanted John Baxter to feel that he's a detective .... I wanted the audience to feel ... maybe doubtful, maybe that they'd missed something, maybe that it didn't happen. And then to think 'Oh, Christ!' and to have the time to get together with their time sense. (Roeg cited in Milne and Houston 1973, p. 3; p. 5)

In the previous chapter, I considered John and Laura's behaviour in *Don't Look Now* as manifestations of anxiety, and suggested that one of the traumas of the film is its sense of complicity in the child's death. In this chapter, however, I want to turn more specifically to the Baxters' fatal misreading of their world and its traumatic consequences. In particular, this chapter draws on Jacques Derrida's concept of *destinerrance*, the sense in which meaning is 'destined to err and to wander' (Miller 2006, p. 897), as a way of understanding the unstable and ultimately horrific process of misreading sign and symbol in *Don't Look Now*. John's misreading of the murderous woman as his lost daughter, but also his misreading of colour and image, of his wife, of the strange psychic women they meet, of himself and his place in the world, of the dangerous spaces he inhabits, and even of time itself, all contribute to the film's uncanny sense of his environment as simultaneously loaded with and empty of meaning. John might 'feel' that he is 'a detective', but ultimately, the film makes clear, he is a failed one, since his misreading of the 'clues' he perceives lead to the perpetuation rather than the prevention of crime and trauma. It is in the space of these misreadings, of failing to see in time, that the film's horror, its capacity to scare, resides, since it insists on the suspension rather than the resolution of trauma. The film's misreadings, then, are ultimately instructive or didactic, but in moving away from the conservative restoration of order which is typical of the Gothic narrative, *Don't Look Now*'s iteration of horror remains open. It is not only John, then, who responds to his horrific mistake as 'Oh God!', but the viewer, too, according to Roeg, who thinks 'Oh, Christ' – both character and viewer call on an ancient figure of authority in response to the film's destabilisation. It is always already, however, too late: John can never be saved from his misreadings. Only the viewer survives to learn from his fundamental errors of judgement. We must not wander, we must not err, the film insists; it is on such failures of knowledge that the film's horror depends.

Destinerrance does not find a fixed abode in Derrida's writing, but J. Hillis Miller has compiled and reflected upon its various iterations as it appears in his numerous works. It is best explained, Miller notes, as a 'spatio-temporal figure' or 'a spatial figure for time. It names a fatal possibility of erring by not reaching a predefined temporal goal in terms of wandering away from a predefined spatial goal' (2006, p. 893). It might therefore be described as *adestination* (2006, p. 895) – a resistance to or the interruption of a fixed or anticipated destination. In its sense of 'delayed action' (ibid.), too, *destinerrance* can also be recognised as affiliated with the disruptive spatial and temporal qualities of trauma, the way in which trauma comes back to haunt, and is only experienced in its belatedness. Perhaps more powerfully for the present study, *destinerrance* is also an anxious concept, since it indicates the lack of control over meaning and signification. Indeed, Miller writes, 'any utterance or writing I make may escape my intentions both as to what it should mean (for others), and as to the destination it is supposed to reach. It may be destined to err and wander, even though it may sometimes, by a happy accident, reach the destination I intended for it' (2006, pp. 896-97). In other words, *destinerrance* might be best understood through the logic of the postcard and its capacity for misreading. As Miller explains:

> The consequences of *destinerred* iterability for everyday life are considerable, to say the least. I write a postcard and send it to my beloved. The postcard means to tell her how much I love her .... A postcard, however, is open to all under whose eyes it happens to fall. Anyone who intercepts it and reads it can take it as addressed to him or to her. Anyone can interrupt its passage to its intended destination. Anyone can short-circuit that passage. Anyone can make my postcard have a meaning I in no way intended .... Iterability also means that the recipient, however fortuitously he or she may come upon that postcard, is transformed into someone else, put beside himself or herself, dislocated, by reading it. I become the person to whom those words seem to be addressed, their fitting recipient. (2006, p. 900)

Destinerrance thus takes on a number of interpretive possibilities in *Don't Look Now*. First, in its capacity for 'wandering', *destinerrance* is recalled in the tourist's wandering (wilful or otherwise) in the labyrinthine city of Venice. For John Baxter, this wandering takes him away from the security of the well-lit streets and into the dark alley of his eventual murder, but it also signifies the way in which he wanders away from rationality.

In pursuing the ghost or doppelgänger of his dead daughter, John claims the figure as destined to meet him. Indeed, the murderer does not pursue John, but rather encourages John to pursue her: she therefore acts as the symbol of *destinerrance* by allowing her victims to read or claim her as their own – she is the 'letter that seems, after the fact, to have been thrown out (*lancée*), at the moment it was written, toward an unknown receiver ....The recipient's "who" is determined at the moment of reception' (2006, p. 895). While the citizens of Venice insistently close their shutters, denying the murderer's presence as being destined for one of them, John does not hesitate to claim himself as the recipient: he 'chances upon the letter' (the murderer, the symbol of his daughter) and 'says, "It is intended for me. It has chosen me, and I choose to be chosen by it. I say, 'It's me (*c'est moi*).'" That might seem to imply that the letter has found its intended recipient. No, the recipient did not exist before receiving the letter. The letter creates the recipient, unpredictably, incalculably, by chance or even by error. The letter reaches that recipient by *destinerrance*' (2006, p. 905). The title of the film certainly indicates this kind of misdirection. As Wisker has it, the title suggests

> ... either the pantomime 'look out behind you!' or indication of something too terrible to endure scrutiny....The object of 'don't look now' is undefined and this and similar phrases of denial or deferral seem always to be wrongly attached to the playful and safe or the potentially threatening. The shifting signifier leaves us uneasy, suggests a lack, a yawning gap in interpretation which is threatening to our sense of stability and security. (1999, p. 26)

However, *destinerrance* also operates in *Don't Look Now* in John's apparent telepathy or capacity for precognition. If the receipt of a telepathic message can be seen to work under the same principles as a form of written communication, then John's gradual realisation of his psychic abilities also constitutes a claim upon a message he believes is destined for him. While this might be true in terms of his anticipation of both his own death and Christine's, John's misreading of the missive occurs when he claims the fleeting figure of the dwarf as part of this psychic discourse. In claiming himself as 'chosen' by the dwarf, the figure of *destinerrance*, John operates under a critical misreading which ensures that his other psychic visions come to fruition.

John's claim on the *destinerrance* of the dwarf and the symbols with which he associates her have often been read as a sign of the film's paranoia. Sanderson, for example, argues that *Don't Look Now* 'creates such an atmosphere of the paranormal and the paranoid that there seems no room for harmless coincidence' (1996, p. 11), while Tony Williams sees such 'paranoid aspects' as 'fundamental components of family horror' (1996, p. 18; see also Houtman 2009). The repetitions of the colour red, for example, in Christine's coat and rubber ball, the 'blood' on the slide, John's own scarf, and the dwarf's coat, most powerfully, suggest critical associations between these images, and which John is determined to read in time, this time.[7] The motif of glass, too, suggests John's pursuit of 'seeing and reflection' (Izod 1992, p. 69; p. 72; pp. 73-74). Other images are not available to John, but are offered up, unexplained, to the viewer, such as the intercut image of the sisters laughing while John and Laura puzzle over their strange assertion that Christine lingers with her parents as a spectral presence (Lanza 1989, p. 116), or the transition from the rain-filled pond to the light-filled window in the opening shots (Patch 2010a, p. 257). Palmer and Riley do observe that *Don't Look Now* 'repeatedly makes strange its own codes of association, undermining one's confidence in interpretation', so that '[w]hat one is left with is very nearly a "floating chain of signifieds," and the result is puzzlement and an uncomfortable sense that both narrative and narration remain "unfixed"' (1995, p. 18; p. 20), while Patch notes that the film's 'elliptical editing style prepares the spectator for a visual strategy that questions our complicit spectatorial passivity in our acceptance of classical narrative structures based around chronology and causality' (2010a, p. 257).[8] However, Roeg's comments on the interpretive work of cinema-viewing suggest that the film's construction of *destinerrance* are more profoundly to do with the deconstruction engaged in by the viewer. In film, he says,

> Thought can be transferred by the juxtaposition of images, and you mustn't be afraid of the audience not understanding. You can say things *visually*, *immediately*, and that's where film, I believe, is going. It's not a pictorial example of a published work, it's transference of thought .... I've always wanted to get my thoughts over in film visually, without the intermediary of literature. I actively *prefer* to be in the cinema, but *not* the cinema of literature, which is like Victorian picture books. (Cited in Kennedy 1980; original emphases)

Although, then, Lawrence Shaffer argues that *Don't Look Now* does too much to make explicit the connections between its image or symbol fragments for the viewer, such as the visual associations between Christine, the gargoyle on the church, and the gnome-like features of the dwarf (1974, p. 7), Roeg's observations about film imagery depend precisely upon the work of *destinerrance*, on a 'transference of thought' which must be claimed by its recipient (the viewer), and not determined by the film or its maker. More than this, argues David Lavery, *Don't Look Now* actively warns us against an assumption of the film's authority, and suggests that this is the key distinction to be made between John and the film's viewer. That is, whereas *Don't Look Now* 'offers us fascinating images but warns us not to give them our assent – warns us to be "*Contre L'Image*"', it is John's misreading of such images as a message or a 'great secret' which 'causes his brutal death' (1983, pp. 52-53).

John does not only misread objects around him as symbols, he also misreads his spatial and temporal environments. Venice, of course, is typically subject to misreadings and misnavigation. In their movement around the shifting city, John and Laura often argue and disagree, each insisting to the other '[w]e've been over this bridge already!' However, for the Baxters, the maze of Venice becomes a paradoxically inhospitable place of work, rest and tourism. Indeed, although at the film's beginning John had appeared relatively fluent in speaking Italian, confidently ordering lunch for himself and his wife in a restaurant, as the film progresses he appears to lose his ability to communicate with ease. His frustration with the hotel staff and the police officers disrupt the clarity of his speech and his understanding of theirs, until by the film's end John speaks to what he believes is a lost Italian child only in English. Not only are both John and Laura made uncomfortable in this inhospitable city, as I explain in more detail in Chapter Four, but from the time of their first meal in Venice John appears to be suspicious of his surroundings. While Laura writes a letter to Johnny, John looks suspiciously around the dining room, fidgeting in his seat and adjusting a nearby window, and while Laura leaves the dining room in order to assist the sisters to find the bathroom, John waits impatiently for her to return. That impatience and discomfort is writ large when Laura leaves Venice for England. While she is gone, and even before he 'sees' her on the funeral barge, John appears lost and 'out of sorts' as he rushes, rather than meanders, around the city – indeed, this is when he falls from the scaffold in the church, distracted, perhaps, from his work.

Time, too, is disrupted and unreadable for John. From the opening sequence in which his attempt to rescue Christine is both rendered in slow motion and repeated, to his sight of Laura on the funeral barge – an event from the future which he reads as occurring in the present – John operates outside a linear sense of time. In one way, this might be read as a kind of traumatic haunting of the present by both past and future. Roeg himself has argued that:

> We are all haunted by our pasts. That's certainly true with most of my characters. You can't escape from the past, and you are always living out your future. But we usually don't know it …. There's no such thing as seeing into the future because the future is already here. A premonition is just a way of confirming something, you know. And I think film is the perfect medium to show this paradox. It's a time machine. (Cited in Lanza 1989, p. 92)

Indeed, this might be recognised as the 'fragile geometry' of John's book, shown in the film's opening scene. However, John's temporal misreadings also suggest the way in which the perception of time is impacted by the experience of trauma in a kind of psychic scarring. Linear time cannot be read by John because for him it no longer exists. For the viewer, too, unable to see beyond John's own experience of the world, these sights can only be read 'as present and factual rather than future and visionary' (Palmer and Riley 1995, p. 21). In his simultaneous memory of trauma and his expectation of its recurrence in the future, John exists both before and after the present moment. Even when, at the film's conclusion, both John and the viewer are shocked into the recognition of these earlier fatal misreadings, all is still not explained.[9] It is never clear, that is, whether the cause of John's temporal disruptions has been supernatural or otherwise (Lanza 1989, p. 98). Even though John has misread the dwarf as a child in danger, and attempted in this way to atone for the past, the conclusion of *Don't Look Now* remains suspended between a supernatural interpretation which posits that he has experienced psychic visions of the future, and an affective interpretation which suggests his anxious preparation for a traumatic return of the past.

It is precisely in terms of this interpretive suspension that John's patriarchal authority and assertions of rationality are undermined or, in other words, that his authority refuses to remain stable, and instead begins to err and wander. This anxiety about gender and social roles is typical of the horror genre (Coulthard and Birks 2016, p. 462; Worland 2007, p. 96). It is the monster which disrupts the 'social equilibrium' of the patriarchy, and in horror films of the late twentieth century, Tony Williams asserts, we come to witness 'various representations of decaying and dissolving male subjects' as a result of what he calls '[p]atriarchal hysteria over masculinity's contemporary dysfunctional condition' (1996, p. 18; p. 20). The monster, he adds, 'often challenge[s] patriarchal family norms', and must bear 'no explicit relationship to everyday life' (1996, p. 21). In one sense, of course, the murderous dwarf is the monster of the film. As I explain later in this chapter and, in a different sense, at the end of Chapter Four, this monster can be seen to operate so far outside John's conceptualisation of femininity (as maternity) that he fails to recognise her as a monster as such. As Wilson puts it, John 'is killed by a woman who refuses to be socially overlooked ... and yet is so radically different from his conception of *woman*, that John can only see her as a helpless child in need of patronising, fatherly protection' (1999, pp. 292-93; original emphasis). However, in terms of acting as a challenge to the 'equilibrium' of John's authority and motivating his 'patriarchal hysteria' the psychic sisters can also be read as figures of monstrosity in *Don't Look Now*. They too differ (or defer) from his understanding of womanhood: as single women travelling without a male companion, they are unreadable, figures of suspicion. Indeed, their depiction in multiple mirrors when Laura first converses with them in the restaurant's bathroom suggests this unreadability and fragmented interpretive possibility.[10] As such, John is quick to accuse them of kidnapping and murder: if Laura has gone missing (as if she is a lost object to be claimed, rather than an independent subject), they must be responsible. In this sense John demonstrates his determination to both protect Laura's passive female role and punish the sisters' active rejection of traditional femininity. Moreover, John's response to both the sisters and the dwarf suggests not only his resolution to return the *destinerred* woman and child (Laura and the dwarf) to their rightful positions within the social order, but also his commitment to punish those who deliberately err from that order (the sisters).

Masculinity in film is typically associated with scopophilia and omnipotence, a power extended from the male protagonist to the film's spectator (Mulvey 1992, p. 24; p. 28). Despite his efforts at the surveillance of the sisters, Laura and the dwarf/child, however, the film's monsters make John weak by causing him fear and uncertainty, disrupting his ability to watch over them. Figures of both mourning and fear in contemporary culture are more usually women or girls; the affective association of these with masculinity is unusual and discomfiting for both character and viewer (Armstrong 2012, p. 2; Hutchings 2009, p. 54). From the moment John fails to rescue his daughter, then, abandoning his physical strength and ability to care for his family in favour of his personal intellectual pursuits, *Don't Look Now* continues to reassert his patriarchal helplessness. Even in the hotel room, Laura mocks John's emaciated frame – his lack of strength. It is not only the women of *Don't Look Now* who err from their traditional roles, then, but John, too. Kinder and Houston suggest that John 'represses his androgyny' (1978, p. 335), Armstrong recognises the infiltration of '"masculine" rationalism' by '"feminine" intuition' (2012, p. 88), and Wilson relates this to 'John's increasing inability to separate his intellectual persona from his new, fear-driven emotional state brought on by his relentless clairvoyance and future-visions' (1999, p. 291).[11] To be sure, John can be seen as feminised by this challenge from both 'monsters' in the film. He might even be seen to be made monstrous himself as a result: Horner and Zlosnik (1999, p. 223) and Wisker (1999, pp. 27-28) argue for John as a third witch, weird sister or fate.[12] Perhaps more particularly, however, this challenge is wrought by John's experience of emotions stereotypically associated with women: fear and anxiety. It is in this shift from the intellectual to the affective that John errs from his patriarchal role.

What all of this amounts to, I argue, is John's fundamental misreading of himself and his place in the (natural and supernatural) world. For Palmer and Riley, '[t]he kinds of seeing and the forms of belief that this rational man ignores or rejects make him vulnerable to his own destructively denied emotions and finally to the force of malevolence in the world' (1995, p. 16), while Lavery argues that John does not know or understand the things he hears or reads (1983, p. 54). More powerfully, perhaps, John actively engages in a physical and psychological rejection of that which confronts his conceptualisation of himself. When the Baxters first meet the sisters, a shot of the blind sister, Heather, is intercut with John's memory of leaving home in the rain; his brief flash of traumatic perception is symbolically denied in the return to the present and Heather's blind eyes. Similarly, after Laura engages in a séance with the sisters, John vomits, something he has not done, he says, for a decade; it is a hysterical response, an abjection of traumatic knowledge. In pushing away any recognition of himself as either (or both) psychic or anxious, John also succeeds in doing the same for the film's audience. In other words, Houtman argues, his hysteria is displaced onto the scene of the film (2009), resulting in the concluding moment of epiphanic horror.

These misrecognitions and misreadings reach their apex in the film's final sequence, particularly as this acts as a fundamental repetition and rereading of its opening scenes.[13] If the work of both John and the viewer has, throughout the film, been to act as a 'detective', then in a terrible completion of the Freudian death drive, it is death which is our ultimate 'reward for learning how to see' (Toles 2013, p. 115). As I suggest throughout this study, *Don't Look Now* is critically driven by John's desire to see and to know in time, this time. Despite the uncanny similarity between Christine and the dwarf, it is not a delusion in which he hopes to save his lost daughter – as I have suggested, John's speech to the hooded figure confirms that he knows this is not his child. Rather, reminded of his failure when he finds a sodden doll on the steps of a canal in Venice, when he sees a drowned woman retrieved from the canal, or a group of small children in red knitted caps, his desire is to save this child as he was not able to save his own. To see John's pursuit of the figure as a death drive, however, is not only to recognise the way in which his emotional development has veered (or wandered) off track, becoming a project of anxiety and anticipation rather than mourning and resolution, but to see this as motivated by his search for 'both forgiveness and punishment at the same time' (Magistrale 2005, p. 108).

In echo of the water-drenched scenes of the opening sequence, the conclusion of *Don't Look Now* is dark, damp and foggy. It evokes what Clover terms the 'Terrible Place' of the slasher movie – the site from which the 'Final Girl' must confront the monster or villain, and which is typically and uncannily dark and damp, or 'intrauterine' (1996, p. 78). In this sense, we might recognise the end of *Don't Look Now* as shifting from the quieter, more psychological horror of its earlier scenes, to the conventions of the slasher or stalker film more typical of 1970s horror cinema. If that is true, then this too speaks not only to John's fatal misreadings in the film, but also to our critical misreading of the film's genre. The inversion of the familiar fairy tale, *Red Riding Hood*, in this final sequence also suggests that misrecognition of the site of threat. The lost, red-hooded figure is pursued through the streets, and while John perceives himself as a saviour (the hunter), his behaviour actually mimics that of the wolf. Indeed, his 'smile' as he attempts to cajole the 'child' is closer to a snarl, as his teeth are bared and his eyes glow in glee that his charge has been trapped. When the figure turns around, however, baring her teeth in her own horrific smile and shaking her head at John for his misreading, *she* is shown to be the wolf, while John cowers in terror, covered or hooded in the red of his own blood.[14]

Figure 6: The 'lost child' is revealed as a murderous dwarf.

Clover, too, has recognised the intertextual play at this point, and reads the dwarf, the Red Riding Hood figure, as the 'Final Girl' (1996, p. 91). This is a move which positions John, of course, as the monster. And although for Clover, the 'Final Girl' is not a feminist figure, Kyle Christensen disagrees; he suggests that Nancy in *A Nightmare on Elm Street* has been seen as the first feminist 'Final Girl' (2011, p. 30), but it might be seen, instead, that the dwarf of *Don't Look Now* fulfils this position. This is, in a sense, a tragic 'reversal of fortune', as Terence Patrick Murphy has it (2008, p. 151). More particularly, however, the concluding sequence of *Don't Look Now* might be read as a kind of revenge on John as symbol of the patriarchal failure which permitted Christine to drown. He is tortured, throughout the film, by his own anxiety, but when he is finally shown his error in claiming himself as saviour rather than as monster, John's pattern of *destinerrance* is complete.

Finally, Laura's responsibility here should not be forgotten. In responding to the sisters' 'message' from Christine, rather than to her husband's apparent psychic and psychological distress, Laura too has misread the situation and failed in her care for others. Just as in the opening sequence she is 'outside the main action' (Sinyard 1991, p. 49), at the end of the film, too, she reaches fruitlessly for John, her warnings coming far too late. Precisely as a result of her insistence that Christine has returned to 'forgive' her parents, rather than to recognise John's capacity for self-punishment, Laura has now lost both her daughter and her husband. It is not only John, then, who has erred, but Laura too. That the film ends with her return to the sisters also suggests, horrifically, that she has not recognised this failure, and has now erroneously claimed the sisters, rather than her remaining family member, Johnny, as her own.

Ultimately, if *Don't Look Now* positions misreading as a product of the wandering of critical interpretation, then it also works as a performance of the patterns of trauma and the ways in which John and Laura fail to read and anticipate danger in time. As a horror film which engages with its own social context, moreover, *Don't Look Now* might also be seen to teach its viewer how to read.[15] Misreading, for both character and viewer, is punished with the horror of revelation; to read correctly is to be confirmed in the pleasure of interpretation.[16] It is not so much, then, that the terror of *Don't Look Now* derives from 'the connections in our lives, connections that we either see or fail to see' (Muir 2002, p. 261), but from the failure to recognise one's own affective responses. If John and Laura were to acknowledge their own trauma and the way in which anxiety structures their engagement with the world, they would guard themselves against the misreadings which secure their terrible fate. But this, of course, would be to engage in a process of mourning. The film depends on the denial in which the Baxters engage, which underpins their anxious behaviour and which permits their *destinerrance*.

FOOTNOTES

7. Readings of the colour red proliferate in the extant criticism. See, for example, Harper and Smith (2012b, p. 166); Izod (1992, pp. 67-68); Lanza (1989, p. 45; p. 99); Palmer and Riley (1995, p. 18); Patch (2010a, pp. 259-60); Patch (2010b, p. 73; p. 77).
8. Schülting, too, adds that *Don't Look Now* 'does not possess a reliable narrational agency, which would help the spectator order these images into a "chrono-logical" story' (1999, p. 199), while Izod argues that the viewer is encouraged to make connections between separate images through the film's intercuts (1992, pp. 68-69). Roeg also notes that this is a function of film editing, observing that 'when you're in the cutting room, you see how drastically you can

change your perceptions and memories by rearranging the order of events. In *Don't Look Now*, you see an old lady, then you see a knife. But we can only infer that it's her knife that stabs the man. Whoever is in charge of editing a film really plays God. It's the juxtaposition of images that changes people's views' (cited in Lanza 1989, pp. 91-92).

9. 'Even with these last frantic moments of revelation, seen through a montage of flashbacks, the story's mosaic, like the one in the church, resists completion' (Lanza 1989, p. 100).
10. Houtman reads this mirror scene as also displaying Laura's misreading of Christine as still alive, arguing that 'Laura is caught in what the film characterises as an imaginary, illusory, and dangerous belief in Christine's survival. It is Laura who is instituted in front of a mirror where she confronts an alienated image of herself, shown literally, when Laura is first talking to the twins in the Gents lavatory; the images of her are fractured, she is splintered into several images, creating incomplete eyelines between herself and the other characters, thus showing the difficulty of human contact' (2009).
11. For Houtman, too, the film 'celebrates masculinity as rational and femininity as chaos' (2009).
12. Hunt notes that the witch has been 'a focal point for the logic of misogyny (historical persecutions), as "implacable enemy of the symbolic order" in the horror film, as representative of male anxiety and/or female power' (2002, p. 89).
13. 'To think of the marvellous ambiguity of the first few minutes of *Don't Look Now* and then of the grand-guignol anticlimax is to weep' (Shaffer 1974, p. 6).
14. Patch offers two interpretations of the proliferation of red at this point in the film. First, he suggests that '[w]hen one considers Christine as the [Kristevan "clean and proper body"], and the dwarf ... as [the abject body], what becomes evident is that red becomes a connection between two disparate bodies, a dyadic relation that positions both bodies at opposite ends of a chromatic spectrum, with one young/innocent/virtuous, the other aged/corrupt/sadistic, a body of innocence and potential lost, contrasted with a body of threat that eventually challenges John's patriarchal position' (2010a, p. 262). Later, he also argues that '[t]he colour draws the viewing experience into a continually evolving mental loop, a connection that at the film's *denouement*, when a resurrected Christine is expected and not delivered ..., heightens the shock at the true nature of the body encountered. Instead of innocence reclaimed, what emerges is a red cosmetic-body that twists the aesthetic connections of grief, loss and reconciliation into the corporeality of corruption and demonic desire' (2010b, p. 78).
15. 'Through this subversion of traditional dramaturgy, the spectator becomes John Baxter's double, believing in what he sees and trying – to no avail however – to reconstruct the images in a chronological and causal order. Thus the spectator in a way shares John Baxter's fate by his or her inability to rationally organise the transitory impressions and to discriminate reality from fantasy as well as the present from the past and the future' (Schülting 1999, p. 200).
16. Murphy, too, argues that *Don't Look Now* teaches us how to read, but relates this to the film's construction as a 'marked order' narrative (2008, p. 151).

Chapter 4: Dereliction and the Trauma of Place

From the haunted house to the graveyard, the foggy night to abandoned ruin, space and place are central to the construction of horror and the Gothic. As I have noted in the introduction, as in the sensation fiction of the 1860s, the horror of 1970s cinema is involved with the way in which the Other is returned to the self, the familiar, the home – in other words, precisely in its uncanniness, its sense of the unhomely. Indeed, as Dwayne Avery has noted, the horror genre might be said to be 'built … on a foundation of aberrant modes of habitation' (2014, p. 4). In *Don't Look Now*, the family home is disturbed by the death of the child; after this event, the family is broken and each member leaves: John and Laura for Venice, Johnny for boarding school. Their home is rendered no longer home, an un-home, by the traumatic event. It is made literally uncanny. Freud's uncanny, Avery argues, 'represents the negation of comfort and security; it is the impossibility of finding home; the uncanny home is a strange and eerie place where the supernatural haunts the dweller; it is a place that abounds in unspeakable horrors and secrets. But, most importantly, the uncanny home rests on repetition; the uncanny is that which should have remained secret but *returns* when the dweller least expects it' (2014, p. 12; original emphasis). In this chapter I want to suggest that the uncanniness of the Baxters' home and the place to which they flee, the transient and liminal space of Venice, is therefore associated with their parental anxiety. These spaces are made uncanny by the return of trauma, that which they should have anticipated but for which they have failed to prepare. More than this, however, it is the cinematic representation of that simultaneous anticipation and return in John's psychic visions which is also uncanny. Precisely in its form as a horror film, 'the uncanniness of history, of people, and of things appears in a space-time that produces singularities and actualises virtual conjunctions' (Löffler 2015, p. 1). Finally, the space of Venice is also rendered uncanny when it is threatened by the monster (the literal murderer as well as the monstrosity of John's anxiety), which persistently disrupts the homely space. In this chapter, then, I attend to the film's settings – the country house and garden (the quintessentially English domestic and pastoral spaces), the hotel (the transient space), the ruined church (the derelict space) and Venice itself (the liminal and labyrinthine space) – for the ways in which these evoke the horror of different kinds of disruption.

I will pay particular attention to the way in which horror invades the family, the heart of the home, but also consider how this is mirrored in the ruined and inhospitable spaces of Venice: the hotel is closing for the season, Laura causes damage in a restaurant, John's restorations on the church are nowhere near completion. Horror, in this film, resides in the ordinary sites of the family, the home, and even the temporal refuge of the holiday. However, dereliction, in this film, also comes to figure Luce Irigaray's conceptualisation of the term as *déréliction* – a description of the way in which women are exiled from the patriarchal community. The chapter concludes, then, by considering Laura, Christine, the psychic sisters, and the monstrous dwarf in terms of their exile and the ways in which this disrupts and makes derelict the spaces which they inhabit.

The film begins, as I have already discussed, on an idyllic representation of an English country house and garden: children happily play, a horse runs wild across the fields, the adults lounge inside a cosy room, chatting and relaxing after their lunch. Despite this tranquil image, the large house, set on spacious grounds, comes to evoke the qualities of the Gothic castle – a grand home in which anything might happen, and the 'setting most overtly evocative of the sins ... associate[d] with the aristocracy' (Cavallaro 2002, p. 29). Indeed, the Baxters do not appear to be an ordinary family: their home, their transatlantic accents, John's unusual occupation and his authorship of an apparently complex book (*The Fragile Geometry of Space*) all point to what Roeg himself has called their 'privilege' (cited in Salwolke 1993, p. 40) – the sense in which they are already unrepresentative of the average film viewer or 'the most avid consumers of Gothic fiction' (Cavallaro 2002, p. 29). 'The tragedy I wanted to show,' Roeg points out, 'was that although there is what appeared to be privilege – they were the golden people – even golden people can't escape life. You know life actually deals the blows' (cited in Salwolke 1993, p. 40). And yet, although the Baxters are initially represented as golden, perfect, untouchable, horror finds its way into their home, already coded as Gothic castle. The grounds are large, to be sure, but they are also wild, unmanicured and unfenced. A wild horse gallops dangerously close to the unsupervised children, glass is hidden in the long grass, and the banks of the deep pond are slippery. The pastoral nostalgia of England's rural past is thus quickly exposed as illusory and even dangerous, so that, as Kristi Wilson has it, even the '"illusory coherence" of the family in their safely isolated home environment (complete with protected boundaries), will soon be exposed' (1999,

p. 283). Isolation does not, however, constitute protection, as the Baxters soon discover. Even the domestic space, assumed to be safe, is infiltrated by the unsafe, the otherness of horror and death. For Wilson, the Baxters' English country house thus constitutes the 'paradoxical geography of failed masculinity' (1999, p. 278). That is, although their 'home and its surrounding landscape is not exactly haunted in a traditionally Gothic manner, every aspect of John's illusory success as a white male professional is haunted by marginal forces which threaten to intrude upon his ability to work and think rationally' (1999, p. 284). This ability to 'work and think' is not limited to John's professional occupation, I argue, but extends to his role as a husband and father. Not only does he fail to adequately answer Christine's question about the curvature of space, replying only (via Laura) that '[n]othing is what it seems', his surveillance of the domestic space, and those within it for whom he is responsible, is lacking. Indeed, that his work has entered the domestic space suggests his failure to demarcate the personal from the professional, just as he has not separated the safe from the unsafe, the family from the foreign Other. That Laura eventually witnesses the horror of her daughter's death from the threshold of their home characterises the way in which the Baxters occupy this liminal space of uncertainty and danger, while deluded about their own safety and security. Her shock and the penetration of her scream from the domestic rural scene to the urban scene of Venice underscores the way in which the Baxters are suddenly exposed to this horror, but prefer to remain under the delusion of their own security. In this way, Wilson adds, 'the strangeness of the Baxters' farm landscape is accentuated by the sharply contrasting climates of England and Venice', so that the 'pastoral images in the Baxters' backyard create a hyperreal atmosphere' (1999, p. 283). Ultimately, one has the sense that it is the security of the domestic scene which is illusory or 'hyperreal', and not the strange visions of the future with which John is preoccupied.

Venice has loomed large in the cultural imagination as a site of liminality, labyrinthine horror, and physical and psychological instability. Indeed, its symbolic value is drawn on so widely and regularly, O'Rawe argues, that it has become a cliché, an overwrought palimpsest of itself; it is, he says, 'a museum without walls that no one needs to visit' (2005, p. 224). In the sense that Venice is, then, both setting and symbolic scene, *Don't Look Now* productively draws on these stereotypes of the city in order to emphasise John's state of uncertainty, not simply with respect to his precognitive visions, but also his disruptive and confusing experience of anxiety. In *Don't Look Now*, Venice is a city of and in peril, as one poster on a crumbling wall in the city reminds us (Sinyard 1991, p. 50), a space of death and decay, even a prison for its traumatised tourists (White 2016, p. 157). Ironically, given the Baxters' 'escape' from their 'haunted house', the apparent place of trauma, Venice comes to figure as the haunted space – this, rather than the site of her death, is where Christine returns (or appears to do so). As a space of haunting and as a space of transition – not only land to sea, East to West, Occident to Orient, but a space of temporariness and tourism more generally – it constitutes a 'liminal realm between reality and phantasy' (Richter 1999, p. 184). Von der Lippe notes, indeed, that 'there is a particular destination fixed at a unique coordinate – geographical, historical, and cultural – which represents for the occidental stranger a confluence of all that is perceived as southern *and* eastern. This magnetic nexus is Venice' (1999, p. 35; original emphasis), while O'Rawe adds that Venice's 'physical vulnerability … only adds to its quasi-mythical status as city and symbol, place and metaphor' (2005, p. 224). For Virginia Richter, in her analysis of Du Maurier's story, this liminality is primarily linked to John's role – or rather, failure – as a tourist. As he and Laura move from day to night in their travel through the city, she posits, they are privy to its transition from the holiday or dream space to a nightmarish vision (Schülting 1999, p. 211; see also Horner and Zlosnik 1999, p. 220); in this transition, 'John now experiences the breakdown of the tourist's constructivist activity: he is no longer able to sustain the received image of a bright, glittering city. His romantic construction collides with a different "reality", a reality, however, that is no more "authentic" than the Venice of honeymoons. The lost tourists now enter the Venice of the Gothic tradition' (Richter 1999, p. 190). O'Rawe, too, observes that 'the Venice of *Don't Look Now* is a wintry place, both literally and metaphorically, and although not entirely devoid of sunshine, it is noticeably devoid of tourists. Its labyrinth of narrow streets and alleys, empty bridges, and still canals are made all the more sepulchral by the film's extensive grey-blue colour palette' (2005, p. 227).

However, the space between 'reality and phantasy' might also be said to describe the experience of anxiety; that is, as I have explained in Chapter Two, the experience of fear in the temporal space both before and after the trauma has occurred, both remembering and anticipating the trauma which has at once occurred and is to come. Indeed, in the sense that these traumatic qualities become associated with the stereotyped Venice, they are already shown to be present in the opening domestic scene; as Sabine Schülting has it, through the 'bleeding' slide, a symbolic representation of the trauma of both John and Christine's deaths, these images 'have come to "invade" England and the soothing fiction of a cosy home, an intact family in beautiful surroundings .... Through the slide, "Venice" or, rather, its semantics already figure as an uncanny presence even before Venice becomes the setting of the story. It violently disrupts the harmony and shatters the illusion' (1999, p. 211). In travelling to Venice, the liminal space, the Baxters make their psychological state geographically and topographically literal: they leave behind the perceived certainty of home and travel to the uncanny and in-between space of the 'floating city'.

Figure 7: The 'bleeding' slide.

More significantly, however, the Baxters are shown to be unaware of the peril of the Venice they inhabit and the threat which perpetually lurks just out of sight: a killer is on the loose, a dead body is pulled from a canal, shutters close firmly on screams heard in the street. They occupy a space of fantasy and delusion, rather than the space of the real, the space of danger.[17] Indeed, the quintessential Venetian blinds (Pfister and Schaf 1999, p. 2) symbolise this 'blindness' for the way in which they both show and hide, and thus for the way in which the gaze is manipulated. If darkness in Gothic texts is 'associated with a psyche unable to perceive where real evil comes from' (Cavallaro 2002, p. 51) and, too, if it is true that the 'point of horror resides in the blind space' (Bontizer cited in

Russell 1998, p. 240), the fact that the film begins with an image of these blinds suggests their symbolic value for the film narrative to come and the Baxters' inability to read Venice as threat until it is too late. Not only does Venice 'resist mapping' (Wisker 1999, p. 28), then, it resists any kind of consistent interpretive reading which might put John and Laura at ease.

It is in this way, too, that Venice is conceptualised as a labyrinth, with a monster at its centre. As the narrative progresses, John and Laura become increasingly lost, not only physically but psychologically. As Magistrale has argued, '[t]he Venetian setting – with its reflective surfaces of water, narrow canals and stone passageways, multiple bridges that John and Laura cross and recross, and pervasive silence – is emblematic of the complex and layered levels of confusion in John's mind. Indeed, the first time Baxter notices the red-hooded figure is at night when Laura and he are lost deep in the bowels of this secreted city' (2005, p. 107). For Cavallaro, too, 'the labyrinth operates simultaneously as a space of punishment symbolic of unresolved fears and as an implicit invitation to understand and accept a view of the human condition as one of perpetual wandering entrapment. Thus, like fear itself, the labyrinth may work as a function of consciousness' (2002, p. 30). In *Don't Look Now*, she adds, the city is associated with epiphany and revelation: it 'is employed as a setting for the exploration of the relationship between the experience of space and notions of discovery and truth' (2002, p. 33). That 'truth' is that John's death, the return of trauma for the Baxter family, is always already fated or foreseen. In the bleeding slide at the film's beginning, the trauma has already been anticipated: not only the trauma of Christine's death, but of John's own. Venice, in its many literary manifestations, is perpetually represented as the city of death. As I have already shown, John misreads these representations and himself in a fantasy of himself as saviour and the 'child' as saved; in the final analysis, however, Venice both exceeds that reading and returns to one which the city is also doomed to anticipate and repeat: Venice as the site of trauma.

Avril Horner and Sue Zlosnik have noted that the use of Venice as setting in Du Maurier's story 'follows the conventions of the classic Gothic tale which frequently uses Italian cities as sites for the exotic, the sinister and the transgressive …. [It] represents the precariousness of "normality": a holiday resort, it is nevertheless haunted by death' (1999, p. 220). These tropes are called up, however, by numerous other Venice narratives, and it is also upon these that the narrative's horrific and uncanny repetition depends. Thomas Mann's *Death in Venice* (1912) begins this cycle: successful author Aschenbach is tortured on his visit to Venice by his sexual and aesthetic obsession with a teenaged boy. His compulsive pursuit of the boy is such that he fails to recognise his own symptoms of a deadly influenza, and dies on the beach while gazing upon the object of his desire. *Death in Venice* was adapted to film by Luchino Visconti in 1971, just two years before the release of *Don't Look Now*. Its association of Venice with death and obsessive pursuit would therefore have been uppermost in the minds of Roeg's audience and its symbolic value was ripe for interpretation. More importantly, however, it positions *Don't Look Now* as a repetition of those traumas. Both films are therefore always already looking both forward and back to the originary trauma and its later repetition, both remembering and anticipating its horror. This cycle continues throughout the later part of the twentieth century. Martin McDonagh's film *In Bruges* (2008) and Ian McEwan's novel *The Comfort of Strangers* (1981; adapted to film by Paul Schrader in 1990) also recall these tropes; in particular, the former makes reference to *Don't Look Now* in its misreading of a dwarf as a child, while the latter makes use of the emotionally damaged couple who are lured to their deaths by an apparently innocent figure.

In its symbolism and its repetition, Venice is therefore perpetually represented as an uncanny space. This uncanniness, in *Don't Look Now*, can also be read as a function of its decay, and the logic of the ruin. John's occupation involves the restoration of derelict buildings, and it is for this reason the Baxters have ostensibly come to Venice. But more than this, his work highlights the trauma symbolised by the ruin and the way in which it circumscribes and describes their behaviour. Dylan Trigg has argued that 'the place of trauma and the subject of trauma form a structurally parallel unity' (2009, p. 88). For him, ruins designate the 'location of memory, in which trauma took place and continues to be inextricably bound with that location in both an affective and evidential manner. Note, however, that a ruin does not have to involve a relationship with the built environment ...."[N]atural" environments can become materially altered by the events that occurred there' (2009, p. 88). In *Don't Look Now*, we might, then, describe the Baxters' own home and garden in terms of the traumatised ruin. The safety of the domestic space and of the rural idyll has been 'ruined' by the irruption of trauma. As I have suggested, however, the trauma which occurs in the film's opening scene is not simply the trauma of Christine's death; rather, it is also constituted by John's anticipation of his own death, and the structural anxiety (the anticipation of the traumatic return) which pervades the scene. As Trigg has it, in its collapse of past and present, the ruin not only testifies to trauma, to the building's own destruction (2009, p. 96), but also makes clear the way in which trauma operates, that 'it is only when conflicting temporalities are brought together, so constituting a single non-linear timescale, that trauma becomes pronounced as such' (2009, p. 93). The ruin, therefore, like the process of anxiety, holds trauma in suspense, as symbol of both past and future.

The hotel in which the Baxters stay while in Venice is not a welcoming home-away-from-home, but an inhospitable space which emphasises the transience of the artificial domestic space. It is, in a sense, a ruin of the domestic space – a fitting retreat for a couple mourning the ruin of their family. Like Venice, the hotel is, of course, a tourist space, set aside for those who are outsiders, those who do not belong. Like the city itself, the hotel is established as out of season, 'desolate because it is empty, closed up, hostile to intruders' (Milne 1973, p. 238). Indeed, at every turn the Baxters are denied the comfort of home. The hotel is shown as two spaces: the lobby and the Baxters' room. The lobby is not a site of welcome. Although this might be said to be true of hotel lobbies in general – as Trigg has it, they are 'cold places, not fit for habitation' (2006, p. 161) – the hotel of *Don't Look Now* takes this to the extreme.

Figure 8: The hotel lobby.

Roeg famously cast in *Don't Look Now* an Italian film critic as a hotel manager who does not like his guests (Milne and Houston 1973, p. 3). More than this, however, this is a hotel which does not like its guests, which resists its guests' repose. Thus the furniture in the lobby is covered with white sheets – 'ghostly sheets', as Toles reads them (2013, p. 123) – denying the comfort of a hotel guest who might care to sit down, and signalling the hotel's imminent closure. Even the doors are blocked by this rearranged furniture and a pile of rolled rugs: do not enter, the room suggests, little thinking that some guests might remain to exit. The Baxters, it is clear, have outstayed their welcome. Trigg argues that transient space, like the hotel lobby, 'encourages motion and not repose. We are led to pass through it'. Importantly, he adds '[w]hen we do seek motionlessness in motion-bound space, anxiety is the likely result' (2006, p. 161). Roeg, too, has said that characters who do not '*meld* with their environment', those who are '[i]n an unfamiliar place … can't help relating differently …. In a strange place you have to keep rechecking reality. It's not quite the same' (cited in Kennedy 1980; original emphasis). Thus, after Laura has left the hotel in order to tend to their son in England, John's enforced stillness in the hotel increases his anxiety. He paces the floor, demands the assistance of the hotel manager, and becomes paranoid about Laura's safety. This anxiety might also be seen, however, in John's earlier behaviour in the couple's hotel room. Although it might seem that one's room would offer a sanctuary not established in the lobby, the Baxters' room puts the lie to that assumption. Any comfort the Baxters attempt to establish is repeatedly disrupted: a maid enters the room without invitation while John (naked) attempts to work; a telephone call comes in the middle of the night, interrupting the couple's sleep; and even their love-making is disrupted by the intercut scenes of their later lives. The room also becomes messy and uncomfortable: after the couple makes love, Laura strips the bed of its sheets, but finds nowhere to leave them, instead draping them awkwardly in the bathroom, foreshadowing the sheets which cover the furniture in the lobby through which they are about to pass; she sits awkwardly in the too-small bath, legs crossed, rather than in a reclined or relaxed position; while John waits for Laura to dress for dinner, he must perch uncomfortably on the bed with his drink, rather than sit in a chair; and as John packs his belongings to leave the city, he finds their detritus strewn over the bathroom – he cannot pack a tube of toothpaste which has lost its lid, and leaves it to fester. The cumulative effect is not only of discomfort, but of domestic ruin. The Baxters can find no place for rest and repose and are not only left without their daughter, but without a home. Indeed, the one follows the other: home, now, is impossible. Trigg argues that the 'distinction between being at home and finding a dwelling in which we can shelter is centred on the conflict involving being in a familiar space yet not owning that space'. In the latter, 'repose is threatened by a lack of continuity' (2006, p. 161). Since any continuity between the Baxters' former life as a family and their current nomadic existence has been disrupted, both John and Laura are unable to relax. Instead, they maintain a high emotional key: the hotel and the city of Venice only increase their anxiety. What is more, he adds, while 'inside space is closely aligned with intimacy … the outside is posited as being in hostile conflict with intimacy' (2006, p. 162). Since, as I have shown, even the Baxters' intimacy is disrupted in the hotel space, it might be seen that here the outside has entered inside. As the hotel packs up and attempts to shut down, the derelict city enters the otherwise protected space of the hotel, and its dereliction, too, enters the lives of the Baxters.

The hotel is not the only derelict space in *Don't Look Now*. The ostensible reason for the Baxters' visit to Venice involves John's work in restoring an old church in the city (in Du Maurier's story, in contrast, the couple are on holiday). This church is first seen on a slide in the Baxters' home, as John prepares for their visit. For Wilson, this initial introduction to the building and to the city suggests John's detachment from his work (rational rather than spiritual), as well as from his own psychic abilities; '[f]rom a comfortable non-urban setting', she argues, 'John gazes upon the urban space he is attempting to restore from afar', and even though he uses his magnifying instruments, he cannot recognise the strange red figure which appears in one of the church pews (1999, p. 286). Certainly, it is true that the church is seen here only in the abstract, as work, in miniature and in part rather than as a grand narrative of spirituality which might explain some of John's strange visions. What should not be overlooked, however, is the damage done to the slide in this early scene. When John spills water on the slide, not only does the disturbed red ink look like blood: in addition, the slide is ruined and the (image of the) church is reinforced as derelict. The warning, then, is not only that blood will be spilled, but more precisely to do with the ruin as a figure of trauma, anxiety, and troubled space. As 'blood' spills across the image of the ruined church, so too does trauma emerge from, and in, the ruined space of the home and of Venice.

This church is not, however, the first one we see the Baxters visit in Venice. After her brief hospital stay, Laura insists that the couple stop at a church so that she can say a prayer for Christine. While Laura lights a candle, John plays with a broken light switch; the contrast between their rational and spiritual beliefs is clear, and has often been commented upon in the extant criticism. What has not been addressed, however, is the contrast between this church and the church on which John works. While his church is derelict and in need of restoration, this church is busy, a site for tourists – indeed, it is here the Baxters see the psychic sisters on a tour of the church. This church is, then, a tourist site, a façade, rather than a site of real engagement with the past or with something otherworldly. In other words, this is the mask of tourist Venice, beneath which the Baxters ultimately peer: they see the ruin beneath the façade, just as the film as a whole exposes the traumatic ruin beneath the façade of the beautiful couple and the happy family.

The church on which John works is shown from both inside and outside. The outside is brittle, stained and decaying. John is shown perched on a scaffold, face to face with a hideous gargoyle he is attempting to fix more securely to the wall, his own garish grin a mirror to the carving. It is a foreshadowing of his final meeting with the dwarf, the monster at the centre of the labyrinth, to be sure, but in the sense that his face mimics the gargoyle's, the face of the ruin, the shot also suggests the way in which John himself is a ruin, a reflection of traumatised space. Inside, too, he balances precariously on a scaffold, meticulously matching tiny mosaic tiles. In both cases, John is shown to be face to face with history, attempting to restore the past. But if the church is a symbol of the old world, of history both ancient and more recent, that history is also shown to be impossible to access at best, and false at worst. As Izod argues, 'while *Don't Look Now* can be read as reworking ancient mysteries to revitalise them for the present day, it shows churches as repositories of only the merest vestiges of those mysteries. Rendered in monumental stone, they have ossified and decayed, and no longer represent divine power' (1992, p. 76). Just as John attempts to restore the church, so too he attempts to restore his family.[18] What he fails to recognise, however, is that he cannot, anxious subject, defend against trauma's return.

Figure 9: John works on the church façade, face to face with history.

This point is underscored by John's near-death fall from the scaffold inside the church. Trigg has suggested that the act of ascending a staircase signifies a progress to knowledge (2006, p. 165). '[S]taircases that do not reward ascent,' he adds, 'tend to be memorable, if only because they purport to negate their supposed essence' (2006, p. 166). In this sense, the scaffold anticipates the precarious stairs which John climbs at the film's end, only to come face to face with his murderer, and the trauma he had attempted to allay. In the case of both the scaffold and the stairs, John pursues knowledge and the restoration of order; in both cases, however, he falls. In each fall, finally, John is exposed to his fundamental error and the false confidence in his own knowledge. The fall from the ruined scaffold and stairs symbolises the way in which the ruin, the trauma space, has undermined John's pursuit of rationality and order, leaving him in the site of trauma and dereliction.

Throughout this chapter I have used the term 'dereliction' as synonymous with the figure of the ruin, signifying architectural and urban collapse and disorder. As *déréliction*, however, the term has also been adopted to describe women's relationship to the social order. Irigaray uses *déréliction* to describe women's lack of independent subjectivity; women, she argues, are only ever positioned as mother, their social role limited to the maternal function. Margaret Whitford argues that this is a purposeful patriarchal move, designed to ensure women are kept dependent and remain in the private sphere (1991,

Figure 10: John falls from the scaffold inside the church.

p. 153). In other words, women are positioned in 'a state of *déréliction*' so that they do not threaten the 'patriarchal, symbolic order' (1991, p. 77). *Déréliction*, in recalling the ruin, suggests for Irigaray women's homelessness 'in the symbolic order'; there is no place for women outside of the mother or maternal function (1991, p. 125, p. 80). This *déréliction* of women has an important impact on the relationships between mothers and daughters. Since the only available place for a woman is the place of the mother, in an act of 'vertical violence' the daughter is compelled to compete for her mother's role, and must symbolically 'murder' the mother in order to take her position. The contrast to that vertical violence is 'a horizontal relation' – in other words, a female community which counters the patriarchal limitation on women's social roles (1991, p. 78). What I want to suggest is that in addition to the kinds of architectural ruin I have addressed here, and which signify the visual representation of trauma and anxiety, *Don't Look Now* also articulates the social ruin of women's *déréliction*, as well as its counter. It is in this sense that John's death can be understood as a reversal of the symbolic order and a kind of revenge on the symbolic father.

All of the women of *Don't Look Now* might be described in terms of Irigaray's *déréliction*. Christine, of course, is prevented from attaining the role of mother (the only role permitted to her in the symbolic order) by her premature death. That she abandons her doll (her surrogate child) for the ball might also suggest her early failure in this role, and the narrative's punishment of her for this failure as such. The dwarf, too, appears to be acting in revenge against the inhabitants of the city for her own *déréliction*: in behaving as a lost child, she mocks the maternal care of those whom she lures to their deaths. The psychic sisters also operate outside of the maternal function, travelling without male companions and caring only for one another. Although they do mimic a performance of maternity in their small collection of photographs and a tiny bust of the children in their family, ultimately the sisters exist in a state of *déréliction* into which they also draw Laura, lost, too, now, without her daughter and even without her still-living son. But if Venice is the space of dereliction, it is not a site of homelessness for such women; rather it is their site of safety, a space sympathetic to their social position. Indeed, as Palmer and Riley have observed, Heather, the blind and psychic sister, feels safer in Venice than she does elsewhere: although others might become lost in the labyrinthine streets, she is able to hear and sense her way through the city (1995, p. 15). Moreover, in his reading of Du Maurier's story, von der Lippe argues that her adaptation, as it were, of Mann's *Death in Venice* comprises a shift from the 'single male protagonist to a married couple', which in turn 'draws attention to the man's vulnerability when inside the labyrinth, compared with the woman's relative strength and self-possession' (1999, p. 40). Indeed, he adds, it is the women who are strongest in this narrative: it is they 'who traverse the labyrinth with relative ease and confidence, who survive where men cannot' (1999, p. 45). What I want to suggest, then, is that, giving new meaning to the police inspector's observation that while men become more distinct as they grow older, women converge, these *dérélict* women form a horizontal relation, a new community, which reacts against John, symbol of the patriarchal values which make them *dérélict* in the first place.[19] Laura is repeatedly at the centre of a struggle between John and the two sisters: she leaves him alone at the church in order to follow them; when he 'sees' the three on the funeral barge his shouts are ignored or unheard; at the film's end, Laura walks in mourning garb into a church, flanked by the sisters; and, of course, his insistence that Christine is dead is pitted against their assertion that she is still with her parents. The unexplained shot of their laughter intercut with an argument between John and Laura further underscores their pattern of undermining his patriarchal authority over his wife. What is more, the dwarf might be seen to be acting in (unconscious) concert with the sisters, luring John to his death as they lure Laura away from her symbolic role as mother and into horizontal relation with other women. Not only, then, can John's death be seen as 'a manifestation of patriarchal anxiety', so that 'John is killed by the "phallic" mother', as Horner and Zlosnik have it; '[t]hat is, John is killed by what has been repressed within Western culture, a system whose values have constructed his own' (1999, p. 227). More than this, in this new structural order, the dwarf might be seen to act as a kind of God who judges and casts out John when he is found wanting.

Figure 11: The sisters' unexplained laughter.

Don't Look Now's depiction of the derelict and uncanny spaces of urban Venice, the pastoral home, the transient space of the hotel and the ruined space of the church, not only act as symbolic and structural figurations of the Baxters' psychological trauma, they also anticipate the social *déréliction* of the film's women. In doing so, *Don't Look Now* marks a critical relationship between the trauma of the bereaved parent and the 'homelessness' of women in contemporary society. This alignment ultimately situates not only John, but also the dwarf, as acting from the site of trauma, thereby troubling the moral ground of the horror film and moving it away from the conservative order traditionally promoted by the Gothic narrative. *Don't Look Now*, as representative of the disruptive potentialities of 1970s horror, leaves us unsettled, even *dérélict*, as it divides our sympathies and traumatically interrupts our moral relation to the text.

FOOTNOTES

17. 'This "perturbed realism" is clearly manifested in the way space is handled in most horror movies. The story will promise as "real" (unthreatened) space, identified with and inhabited by the normal characters, which becomes violently disrupted whenever the monster figure enters the frame via a suspenseful alternation of the monster's on-screen presence and absence' (Russell 1998, p. 240).
18. Armstrong, too, argues that 'John's work constitutes a sublimated attempt to restore the past, to pretend that it has not gone, that nothing has changed' (2012, p. 89), and Sinyard has suggested that 'Baxter's restoration of the church might be seen as analogous to his attempt to restore his married life to some semblance of order, but religion, faith, prophecy give no meaning to his life. Accordingly, the film's religious aspect emphasises, by contrast, the meaninglessness of Baxter's death' (1991, p. 51).
19. For Lanza, too, 'Laura Baxter and the Scottish sisters represent a matriarchal connivance working to exclude John from the hermetic death-birth process involving his daughter' (1989, p. 45).

CONCLUSION: *DON'T LOOK NOW* AND THE CINEMA OF TRAUMA

In the concluding chapter of her quintessential study of trauma theory, *Unclaimed Experience*, Cathy Caruth describes a story related by Freud in *The Interpretation of Dreams* (1899). In the story, a father has been watching over his sick child for a number of days, until the child dies. Exhausted, the father falls asleep in the next room, only to dream that his son is still alive, and calling to him in distress: 'Father, don't you see I'm burning.' The father awakens and hurries to his child, to find that a candle has fallen and set part of his body alight (Caruth 1996, p. 93). For Freud, Jacques Lacan and Caruth herself, the tale provokes a number of readings to do with the parent's response to the trauma of the loss of the child. Freud, for example, posits that to stay within the dream 'delays his response to the waking reality ... *why dream rather than wake up?*' (1996, p. 94; original emphasis). In this respect, the answer is to do with the dream as wish-fulfilment: 'If the father dreams rather than wakes up, it is because he cannot face the knowledge of the child's death while he is awake' (1996, p. 95). Later, however, Freud proposes another interpretation: that the father's wish to sleep can be seen as his consciousness's desire for its own suspension — in other words, a temporary reprieve from the awful knowledge of the child's death (1996, p. 96). Where Freud asks about the father's sleep, however, Lacan considers the function of his awakening, '[f]or if the dreamer's awakening can be seen as a response to the words, to the address of the child, within the dream, then the awakening represents a paradox about the necessity and impossibility of confronting death. As a response to the child's request, the plea to be seen, the father's awakening represents not only a responding, that is, but a missing, a bond to the child that is built upon the impossibility of a proper response' (1996, p. 100). What this means, in other words, is that '[t]o awaken is thus precisely to awaken only to one's repetition of a previous failure to see in time ... *Awakening*, in Lacan's reading of the dream, *is itself the site of a trauma*, the trauma of the necessity and impossibility of responding to another's death' (ibid.; original emphasis). The story's paradox, then, is that in order 'to see the child's living vulnerability as it dies, the father has to go on dreaming. In awakening, he sees the child's death too late, and thus cannot truly or adequately respond' (1996, p. 103).

The logic of Freud's story can be usefully applied to the discursive structures of trauma and anxiety in *Don't Look Now*. For John to continue to 'see' his daughter is, in effect, to go on dreaming, like the father in Freud's tale. For him to disbelieve the sisters and deny the presence of Christine's 'ghost' would be for him to wake up, just as he awoke from his reverie on seeing the bleeding slide at home at the film's beginning. What this means is that John effectively remains 'asleep' throughout the film – if to awaken is to survive, to bear witness to his failure to see, John remains wilfully asleep, ignorant of the seeing and knowing of his own death which he could anticipate is to come. To awaken to this knowledge would be to gain his own survival. The moment of horror, for both John and the audience, then, is in attaining that knowledge too late: in once again awakening too late. In the final analysis, as Caruth puts it, '[t]o awaken is thus to bear the imperative to survive: to survive no longer simply as the father of a child, but as the one who must tell *what it means not to see*, which is also what it means to hear the unthinkable words of the dying child' (1996, p. 105; original emphasis). When we finally see John 'awaken', we know, horrifically, what it is '*not to see*', what we have not looked at, now, throughout the film.

Throughout this book, I have considered *Don't Look Now* through various discourses of trauma, with a particular focus on anxiety. Moreover, this discussion has depended on a critical paradox of trauma:

> that the most direct seeing of a violent event may occur as an absolute inability to know it; that immediacy, paradoxically, may take the form of belatedness. The repetitions of the traumatic event – which remain unavailable to consciousness but intrude repeatedly on sight – thus suggest a larger relation to the event that extends beyond what can simply be seen or what can be known, and is inextricably tied up with the belatedness and incomprehensibility that remain at the heart of this repetitive seeing. (1996, pp. 91-92)

In other words, trauma is described by the way in which it can only be known afterwards, or too late, through the logic of *Nachträglichkeit* (afterwardsness). Prior to this moment of revelation, the trauma sufferer may involuntarily see or experience the traumatic event again (via the repetition compulsion), but they will fail to understand it as such. As I have just suggested, the trauma in *Don't Look Now* is precisely to do with the horror of simultaneously seeing and failing to see, of looking now and looking too late. The horror of *Don't Look Now* resides in the trauma of failing to know and thus to respond in time, of failing to be responsible. At the film's conclusion, then, both character and audience align in this awful knowledge, the horror of their own failure to read the experience or the narrative correctly. All of this is to say that *Don't Look Now* has as much to say about the cinema of trauma as it does the cinema of horror. Indeed, Roeg's film brings the two precisely into relation with one another; in doing so, the film makes a commentary on the cultural traumas of the late twentieth century, as well as the ways in which these function more particularly as anxiety – an anticipation of the return of trauma, rather than solely as its repetition.

Trauma cinema is most often associated with cinema of the Holocaust (for example, *Schindler's List* [dir. Steven Spielberg, 1993]), as well as films about abuse and 'recovered memory', typically linked with Dissociative Identity Disorder (as in, for example, *Sybil* [dir. Daniel Petrie, 1977]). Indeed, cinema is particularly suited to the trauma narrative because 'it allows us to "incorporate" unsighted horrific scenes in our memory, to "behead" or distort the horror it mirrors, and to influence the discourse about violent events in real life' (Köhne, Elm and Kabalek 2014, p. 2), and because it offers a 'key means for the narrative temporalisation of experience in the twentieth century, and its specific stylistic devices (*mise en scène*, montage, conventions for marking point of view and temporal shifts in particular) have made it a cultural form closely attuned to representing the discordances of trauma' (Luckhurst 2008, p. 177). Indeed, modern cinema was developed around the same time as psychoanalysis and its neuroses of trauma, and the two have continued to interact and influence one another into the present day (ibid.). To recognise horror cinema as the cinema of trauma, however, is not only to recognise the way in which horror calls up 'the intense feelings of fear, shock and disgust that are associated with "trauma"' (Köhne, Elm and Kabalek 2014, p. 3), but to consider the ways in which these feelings have individual and social impact. Although horror is typically seen as a 'low' genre, then, to see it in the light of trauma cinema is to recognise its more profound cultural discourses. Indeed, as Linnie Blake has it, 'horror film … is uniquely situated to engage with the insecurities that underpin … conceptions of the nation; to expose the terrors underlying everyday national life and the ideological agendas that dictate existing formulations of "national cinemas" themselves' (2008, p. 9).

E. Ann Kaplan and Ban Wang have outlined four different impacts trauma cinema can have on its viewer: it can act as a comfort or a cure for the trauma; it can leave the viewer traumatised or shocked; it can allow the viewer to act as a voyeur; and it can offer the viewer the opportunity to bear witness to trauma (2004, pp. 9-10). It is this last which is most ethical and most culturally productive, they argue, for it is only in encouraging the viewer to bear witness to trauma that it can promote compassion and, I would add, responsibility. What Luckhurst calls 'traumatic impact' (2008, p. 180), then, can also be seen in terms of the social and individual impacts of the cinemas of horror and trauma. For *Don't Look Now* to consider the ways in which we must not only look forward rather than back, but precisely acknowledge ourselves as doing so in a process of survival, is to productively engage with the film's horror and its traumatic impact.

Don't Look Now is not, then, simply a film of horror, of grief, of trauma, of mourning, of anxiety. It is a film which brings all of these prominent affects of the late twentieth century into relation with one another. In doing so, it invites a reconsideration of the horror film as a literature of responsibility, one which implores us to see and to know even as we desire to turn away.

BIBLIOGRAPHY

Argento, Dario (dir.) 1975, *Deep Red*, Rizzoli Film/Seda Spettacoli.

Armstrong, Richard 2012, *Mourning Films: A Critical Study of Loss and Grieving in Cinema*, McFarland, Jefferson, NC.

Auerbach, Nina 2000, *Daphne Du Maurier: Haunted Heiress*, University of Pennsylvania Press, Philadelphia.

Avery, Dwayne 2014, *Unhomely Cinema: Home and Place in Global Cinema*, Anthem, London.

Barber, Sian 2012, 'Government Aid and Film Legislation: "An Elastoplast to Stop a Haemorrhage"', in Harper and Smith, *British Film Culture in the 1970s*, pp. 10-21.

--- 2009, '"Blue is the Pervading Shade": Re-Examining British Film Censorship in the 1970s', *Journal of British Cinema and Television*, vol. 6, no. 3, pp. 349-69.

Barker, Adam 1992, 'A Suitable Case for Treatment', *Sight and Sound*, vol. 2, no. 6, p. 38.

Berger, Carole 1978, 'Viewing as Action: Film and Reader Response Criticism', *Literature/Film Quarterly*, vol. 6, no. 2, pp. 144-51.

Billson, Anne 2010, '*Don't Look Now*: No 3 Best Horror Film of All Time', *Guardian*, 22 Oct., <https://www.theguardian.com/film/2010/oct/22/dont-look-now-roeg-horror>.

Blake, Linnie 2008, *The Wounds of Nations: Horror Cinema, Historical Trauma and National Identity*, Manchester University Press, Manchester.

Bradley, Peri 2010, 'Hideous Sexy: The Eroticised Body and Deformity in 1970s British Horror Films', in Newland, *Don't Look Now*, pp. 121-30.

Browne, Nick (ed.) 1998, *Refiguring American Film Genres: History and Theory*, University of California Press, Berkeley, CA.

Byron, Glennis, and David Punter (ed.) 1999, *Spectral Readings: Towards a Gothic Geography*, Macmillan, Houndmills.

Canby, Vincent 1973, '*Don't Look Now*, a Horror Tale: Donald Sutherland and Julie Christie in Leads The Cast Suspense Yarn Turns Into a Travelogue', *New York Times*, 10

Dec., <http://www.nytimes.com/movie/review?res=9E0DEFD61239E73ABC4852DFB4678388669EDE>.

Carpenter, John (dir.) 1978, *Halloween*, Compass International.

Carroll, Nöel 2003, 'The General Theory of Horrific Appeal', in Schneider and Shaw, *Dark Thoughts*, pp. 1-9.

--- 1987, 'The Nature of Horror', *Journal of Aesthetics and Art Criticism*, vol. 46, no. 1, pp. 51-59.

Caruth, Cathy 1996, *Unclaimed Experience: Trauma, Narrative, and History*, Johns Hopkins University Press, Baltimore, MD.

Cavallaro, Dani 2002, *The Gothic Vision: Three Centuries of Horror, Terror and Fear*, Continuum, London.

Champlin, Charles 1976, 'The Films of Nicolas Roeg', *Spectator*, 9 Oct., pp. 26-27, <http://archive.spectator.co.uk/article/9th-october-1976/26/the-films-of-nicolas-roeg>.

Cherry, Brigid 2009, *Horror*, Routledge, London.

--- 2002, 'The Return of the Repressed? British Horror's Heritage and Future', in Chibnall and Petley, *British Horror Cinema*, pp. 1-9.

Chibnall, Steve, and Julian Petley (ed.) 2002, *British Horror Cinema*, British Popular Cinema, Routledge, London.

Christensen, Kyle 2011, 'The Final Girl versus Wes Craven's *A Nightmare on Elm Street*: Proposing a Stronger Model of Feminism in Slasher Horror Cinema', *Studies in Popular Culture*, vol. 34, no. 1, pp. 23-47.

Clover, Carol J. 1996, 'Her Body, Himself: Gender in the Slasher Film', in Grant, *The Dread of Difference*, pp. 66-113.

Cocks, Jay 1973, 'Cinema: Second Sight', *Time*, 10 Dec., <http://www.time.com/time/magazine/article/0,9171,908304-1,00.html>.

Cooper, Ian 2016, *Frightmares: A History of British Horror Cinema*, Auteur, Leighton Buzzard.

Coulthard, Lisa, and Chelsea Birks 2016, 'Desublimating Monstrous Desire: The Horror of Gender in New Extremist Cinema', *Journal of Gender Studies*, vol. 25, no. 4, pp. 461-76.

Cowie, Elizabeth 2003, 'The Lived Nightmare: Trauma, Anxiety, and the Ethical Aesthetics of Horror', in Schneider and Shaw, *Dark Thoughts*, pp. 25-46.

Craven, Wes (dir.) 1996-2011, *Scream* Franchise, Dimension Films.

--- 1984, *A Nightmare on Elm Street*, New Line Cinema.

Creed, Barbara 1998, 'Film and Psychoanalysis', in John Hill and Pamela Church Gibson (ed.), *The Oxford Guide to Film Studies*, Oxford University Press, Oxford, pp. 77-90.

--- 1993a, 'Dark Desires: Male Masochism in the Horror Film', in Steven Cohan and Ina Rae Hark (ed.), *Screening the Male: Exploring Masculinities in Hollywood Cinema*, Routledge, London, pp. 118-33.

--- 1993b, *The Monstrous-Feminine: Film, Feminism, Psychoanalysis*, Routledge, London.

de Lauretis, Teresa 1984, *Alice Doesn't: Feminism, Semiotics, Cinema*, Palgrave Macmillan, Houndmills.

De Palma, Brian (dir.) 1978, *The Fury*, 20th Century Fox.

--- 1976, *Carrie*, United Artists.

Decker, Lindsey 2016, 'British Cinema is Undead: American Horror, British Comedy and Generic Hybridity in *Shaun of the Dead*', *Transnational Cinemas*, vol. 7, no. 1, pp. 67-81.

Dempsey, Michael 1974, 'Rev. *Don't Look Now*', *Film Quarterly*, vol. 27, no. 3, pp. 39-43.

Dika, Vera 1990, *Games of Terror: Halloween, Friday the 13th, and the Films of the Stalker Cycle*, Associated University Presses, Cranbury, NJ.

Donner, Richard (dir.) 1976, *The Omen*, 20th Century Fox.

Downing, Lisa 2011, 'On the Fantasy of Childlessness as Death in Psychoanalysis and in Roeg's *Don't Look Now* and von Trier's Antichrist', *Lambda Nordica*, vol. 2, no. 3, pp. 47-68.

Du Maurier, Daphne 2006, *Don't Look Now and Other Stories*, Penguin, Harmondsworth.

Forrest, David 2013, *Social Realism: Art, Nationhood and Politics*, Cambridge Scholars, Newcastle upon Tyne.

Franklin, Richard (dir.) 1978, *Patrick*, Filmways.

Fraser, Peter 2015, *A Christian Response to Horror Film: Ten Films in Theological Perspective*, McFarland, Jefferson, NC.

Freud, Sigmund 1936, *Inhibitions, Symptoms and Anxiety*, Alix Strachey (trans.), International Psychoanalytical Library 28, Hogarth, London.

Friedkin, William (dir.) 1973, *The Exorcist*, Warner Bros.

Gallagher, Mark 2004, 'Tripped Out: The Psychadelic Film and Masculinity', *Quarterly Review of Film and Video*, vol. 21, no. 3, pp. 161-71.

Gildersleeve, Jessica 2014, *Elizabeth Bowen and the Writing of Trauma: The Ethics of Survival*, Brill/Rodopi, Amsterdam and New York

Gomez, Joseph 1981, 'Another Look at Nicolas Roeg', *Film Criticism*, vol. 6, no. 1, pp. 43-54.

Grant, Barry Keith (ed.) 1996, *The Dread of Difference: Gender and the Horror Film*, Texas Film Studies, University of Texas Press, Austin.

Hantke, Steffan 2007, 'Academic Film Criticism, the Rhetoric of Crisis, and the Current State of American Horror Cinema: Thoughts on Canonicity and Academic Anxiety', *College Literature*, vol. 34, no. 4, pp. 191-202.

Harper, Sue 2010, 'Keynote Lecture, Don't Look Now: British Cinema in the 1970s Conference, University of Exeter, July 2007', in Newland, *Don't Look Now*, pp. 23-28.

Harper, Sue, and Justin Smith 2012a, 'Introduction', in Harper and Smith, *British Film Culture in the 1970s*, pp. 1-8.

--- 2012b, 'Technology and Visual Style', in Harper and Smith, *British Film Culture in the 1970s*, pp. 155-72.

--- (ed.) 2012c, *British Film Culture in the 1970s: The Boundaries of Pleasure*, Edinburgh University Press, Edinburgh.

Harrington, Curtis (dir.) 1977, *Ruby*, Dimension Pictures.

Higson, Andrew 1994, 'A Diversity of Film Practices: Renewing British Cinema in the 1970s', in Moore-Gilbert, *The Arts in the 1970s*, pp. 216-39.

Hills, Matt 2005, *The Pleasures of Horror*, Continuum, London.

Hitchcock, Alfred (dir.) 1963, *The Birds*, Universal Pictures.

--- 1960, *Psycho*, Paramount Pictures.

--- 1940, *Rebecca*, United Artists.

--- 1939, *Jamaica Inn*, Mayflower Pictures/Paramount Pictures.

--- 1935, *The 39 Steps*, Gaumont British Distributors.

Hooper, Tobe (dir.) 1974, *The Texas Chainsaw Massacre*, Bryanston Pictures.

Horner, Avril, and Sue Zlosnik 1999, 'Deaths in Venice: Daphne Du Maurier's *Don't Look Now*', in David Punter and Glennis Byron (ed.), *Spectral Readings: Towards a Gothic Geography*, Palgrave Macmillan, Houndmills, pp. 219-32.

Houtman, Coral 2009, 'Cultural Androgyny and Gendered Authorship in *Don't Look Now*', *PsyArt*, 25 Mar. <http://psyartjournal.com/article/show/houtman-cultural_androgyny_and_gendered_authorsh>.

Hunt, Leon 2002, 'Necromancy in the UK: Witchcraft and the Occult in British Horror', in Chibnall and Petley, *British Horror Cinema*, pp. 82-98.

Hutchings, Peter 2009, '"I'm the Girl He Wants to Kill": The "Women in Peril" Thriller in 1970s British Film and Television', *Visual Culture in Britain*, vol. 10, no. 1, pp. 53-69.

Izod, John 1992, *The Films of Nicolas Roeg: Myth and Mind*, St Martin's, New York.

Kaplan, E. Ann, and Ban Wang 2004, 'From Traumatic Paralysis to the Force Field of Modernity', in E. Ann Kaplan and Ban Wang (ed.), *Trauma and Cinema: Cross-Cultural Explorations*, Hong Kong University Press, Hong Kong, pp. 1-22.

Kennedy, Harlan 1983, 'Roeg: Warrior', *Film Comment*, vol. 19, no. 2, pp. 20-23, 80.

--- 1980, 'Bad Timing: Magical Image Slices. Nicolas Roeg – In Interview', *American Cinema Papers*, Jan-Feb. <http://americancinemapapers.homestead.com/files/BAD_TIMING.htm>

Kershner, Irvin (dir.) 1978, *Eyes of Laura Mars*, Columbia Pictures.

Kiersch, Fritz (dir.) 1984, *Children of the Corn*, New World Pictures.

Kinder, Marsha, and Beverle Houston 1987, 'Seeing is Believing: The Exorcist and Don't Look Now', in Gregory A. Waller (ed.), *American Horrors: Essays on the Modern American Horror Film*, University of Illinois Press, Urbana, pp. 44-61.

--- 1978, 'Insiders and Outsiders in the Films of Nicolas Roeg', *Quarterly Review of Film Studies*, vol. 3, no. 3, pp. 317-43.

Kleinhans, Chuck 1974, 'Nicolas Roeg: Permutations without Profundity', *Jump Cut*, vol. 3, <https://www.ejumpcut.org/archive/onlinessays/JC03folder/RoegKleinhans.html>.

Köhne, Julia B., Michael Elm, and Kobi Kabalek 2014, 'The Horrors of Trauma in Cinema', in Michael Elm, Kobi Kabalek and Julia B. Köhne (ed.), *The Horrors of Trauma in Cinema: Violence – Void – Visualisation*, Cambridge Scholars, Newcastle upon Tyne, pp. 1-30.

Kolker, Robert Phillip 1977, 'The Open Texts of Nicolas Roeg ', *Sight and Sound*, vol. 46, pp. 82-84, 113.

Kubrick, Stanley (dir.) 1980, *The Shining*, Warner Bros.

Laine, Tarja 2006, 'Cinema as Second Skin', *New Review of Film and Television Studies*, vol. 4, no. 2, pp. 93-106.

Lanza, Joseph 1989, *Fragile Geometry: The Films, Philosophy, and Misadventures of Nicolas Roeg*, PAJ, New York.

Lapsley, Rob 2009, 'Cinema, the Impossible, and a Psychoanalysis to Come', *Screen*, vol. 50, no. 1, pp. 14-24.

Lavery, David 1983, 'The Horror Film and the Horror of Film', *Film Criticism*, vol. 7, pp. 47-55.

Leach, Jim 2006, '"Everyone's an American Now": Thatcherite Ideology in the Films of Nicolas Roeg', in Lester D. Friedman (ed.), *Fires Were Started: British Cinema and Thatcherism*, 2nd ed., Wallflower, London, pp. 195-208.

Lester, Richard (dir.) 1968, *Petulia*, Warner Bros./Seven Arts.

Lipsitz, George 1998, 'Genre Anxiety and Racial Representation in 1970s Cinema', in Browne, *Refiguring American Film Genres*, pp. 208-32.

Löffler, Petra 2015, 'Ghosts of the City: A Spectrology of Cinematic Spaces', *communication +1*, vol. 4, pp. 1-19.

Luckhurst, Roger 2008, *The Trauma Question*, Routledge, New York.

Mack, Brice (dir.) 1978, *Jennifer*, American International Pictures.

Magistrale, Tony 2005, *Abject Terrors: Surveying the Modern and Postmodern Horror Film*, Peter Lang, New York.

Mank, Gregory William 2014, *The Very Witching Time of Night: Dark Alleys of Classic Horror Cinema*, McFarland, Jefferson, NC.

Mann, Thomas 1998, *Death in Venice and Other Stories*, trans. by David Luke, Vintage, London.

Mayhall, Laura E. Nym 2002, 'Teaching British Cinema History as Cultural History', *Radical History Review*, vol. 83, pp. 193-97.

Mayne, Judith 2002, 'Paradoxes of Spectatorship', in Graeme Turner (ed.), *The Film Cultures Reader*, Routledge, Abingdon, pp. 28-45.

--- 1993, *Cinema and Spectatorship*, Routledge, London.

McDonagh, Martin (dir.) 2008, *In Bruges*, Universal Studies/Focus Features.

McEwan, Ian 1997 (1981), *The Comfort of Strangers*, Vintage, London.

Miller, J. Hillis 2006, 'Derrida's Destinerrance', *MLN*, vol. 121, no. 4, pp. 893-910.

Milne, Tom 1973, 'Rev. Don't Look Now', *Sight and Sound*, vol. 42, no. 4, pp. 237-38.

Milne, Tom, and Penelope Houston 1973, '*Don't Look Now*: An Interview with Nicolas Roeg', *Sight and Sound*, vol. 43, no. 1, pp. 2-8.

Moore, Darrell W. 1983, *The Best, Worst, and Most Unusual: Horror Films*, Beekman House, Wappingers Falls, NY.

Moore-Gilbert, Bart (ed.) 1994, *The Arts in the 1970s: Cultural Closure?*, Routledge, London.

Morgado, Margarida 2002, 'A Loss Beyond Imagining: Child Disappearance in Fiction', *The Yearbook of English Studies*, vol. 32, pp. 244-59.

Muir, John Kenneth 2002, *Horror Films of the 1970s*, vol. I, McFarland, Jefferson, NC.

Mulvey, Laura 1992, 'Visual Pleasure and Narrative Cinema', in *The Sexual Subject: A Screen Reader in Sexuality*, Routledge, London, pp. 22-34.

Murphy, Terence Patrick 2012, '"Almost like a Fairy Tale or Something": Defining the Concept of Neo-Proppian Plot Function in Martin McDonagh's In Bruges', *Style*, vol. 46, no. I, pp. 66-88.

--- 2008, 'Opening the Pathway: Plot Management and the Pivotal Seventh Character in Daphne Du Maurier's *Don't Look Now*', *Journal of Literary Semantics*, vol. 37, pp. 151-68.

Newland, Paul 2010a, 'Introduction: *Don't Look Now*', in Newland, *Don't Look Now*, pp. 11-20.

--- (ed.) 2010b, *Don't Look Now: British Cinema in the 1970s*, Intellect, Bristol.

Newman, Kim 2002, 'Psycho-Thriller, Qu'Est-Ce Que C'est?', in Chibnall and Petley, *British Horror Cinema*, pp. 71-81.

O'Rawe, Desmond 2005, 'Venice in Film: The Postcard and the Palimpsest', *Literature/Film Quarterly*, vol. 33, no. 3, pp. 224-32.

Palmer, James, and Michael Riley 1995, 'Seeing, Believing and "Knowing" in Narrative Film: *Don't Look Now* Revisited', *Literature/Film Quarterly*, vol. 23, no. I, pp. 14-25.

Patch, Andrew 2010a, 'Beneath the Surface: Nicolas Roeg's *Don't Look Now*', in Newland, *Don't Look Now*, pp. 255-64.

--- 2010b, 'Chromatic Borders, Cosmetic Bodies: Colour in the Films of Nicolas Roeg', *Journal of British Cinema and Television*, vol. 7, no. I, pp. 69-81.

Peirse, Alison 2015, 'The Feminine Appeal of British Horror Cinema', *New Review of Film and Television Studies*, vol. 13, no. 4, pp. 385-402.

Petrie, Daniel (dir.) 1976, *Sybil*, Warner Bros. Television Distribution.

Pfister, Manfred, and Barbara Schaff 1999, 'Introduction', in Pfister and Schaff, *Venetian Views, Venetian Blinds*, pp. 1-14.

Pfister, Manfred, and Barbara Schaff (ed.) 1999, *Venetian Views, Venetian Blinds: English Fantasies of Venice*, Rodopi, Amsterdam and New York.

Polanski, Roman (dir.) 1968, *Rosemary's Baby*, Paramount Pictures.

Prince, Stephen 2004a, 'Violence and Psychophysiology in Horror Cinema', in Schneider, *Horror Film and Psychoanalysis*, pp. 241-56.

--- (ed.) 2004b, *The Horror Film*, Rutgers University Press, New Brunswick, NJ.

Quinodoz, Jean-Michel 2005, *Reading Freud: A Chronological Exploration of Freud's Writings*, Routledge, London.

Rashkin, Esther 1992, *Family Secrets and the Psychoanalysis of Narrative*, Princeton University Press, Princeton, NJ.

Richter, Virginia 1999, 'Tourists Lost in Venice: Daphne Du Maurier's *Don't Look Now* and Ian McEwan's *The Comfort of Strangers*', in Pfister and Schaff, *Venetian Views, Venetian Blinds*, pp. 181-94.

Roche, David 2014, *Making and Remaking Horror in the 1970s and 2000s: Why Don't They Do It Like They Used To?*, University Press of Mississippi, Jackson.

Roeg, Nicolas (dir.) 1973, *Don't Look Now*, British Lion Films.

--- 1971, *Walkabout*, 20th Century Fox.

--- 1970, *Performance*, Warner Bros.

Rose, Jacqueline 1976, 'Paranoia and the Film System', *Screen*, vol. 17, no. 4, pp. 85-104.

Russell, David J. 1998, 'Monster Roundup: Reintegrating the Horror Genre', in Browne, *Refiguring American Film Genres*, pp. 233-54.

Salwolke, Scott 1993, *Nicolas Roeg: Film by Film*, McFarland, Jefferson, NC.

Sanderson, Mark 1996, *Don't Look Now*, British Film Institute, London.

Schmoeller, David (dir.) 1979, *Tourist Trap*, Compass International Pictures.

Schneider, Steven Jay (ed.) 2004a, *Horror Film and Psychoanalysis: Freud's Worst Nightmare*, Cambridge Studies in Film, Cambridge University Press, Cambridge.

--- 2004b, 'Manifestations of the Literary Double in Modern Horror Cinema', in Schneider, *Horror Film and Psychoanalysis*, pp. 106-21.

--- 2004c, 'Psychoanalysis in/and/of the Horror Film', in *Schneider, Horror Film and Psychoanalysis*, pp. 1-14.

--- 2004d, 'Toward an Aesthetics of Cinematic Horror', in Stephen Prince, *The Horror Film*, Rutgers University Press, New Brunswick, NJ, pp. 131-49.

--- 2003, 'Murder as Art/The Art of Murder: Aestheticising Violence in Modern Cinematic Horror', in Schneider and Shaw, *Dark Thoughts*, pp. 174-97.

Schneider, Steven Jay, and Daniel Shaw (ed.) 2003, *Dark Thoughts: Philosophic Reflections on Cinematic Horror*, Scarecrow Press, Lanham, MD.

Schrader, Paul (dir.) 1990, *The Comfort of Strangers*, Skouras Pictures.

Schülting, Sabine 1999, '"Dream Factories": Hollywood and Venice in Nicolas Roeg's *Don't Look Now*', in Pfister and Schaff, *Venetian Views, Venetian Blinds*, pp. 195-212.

Shaffer, Lawrence 1974, 'Night for Day, Film for Life', *Film Quarterly*, vol. 28, no. 1, pp. 2-8.

Shail, Robert (ed.) 2008, *Seventies British Cinema*, Palgrave, Houndmills.

Sinyard, Neil 1991, *The Films of Nicolas Roeg*, Charles Letts, London.

Smith, Angela M. 2011, *Hideous Progeny: Disability, Eugenics, and Classic Horror Cinema*, Columbia University Press, New York.

Smith, Justin 2014, 'Calculated Risks: Film Finances and British Independents in the 1970s', *Historical Journal of Film, Radio and Television*, vol. 34, no. 1, pp. 85-102.

Smuts, Aaron 2009, 'Art and Negative Affect', *Philosophy Compass*, vol. 4, no. 1, pp. 39-55.

Sobchack, Vivian 1996, 'Bringing it All Back Home: Family Economy and Generic Exchange', in Grant, *The Dread of Difference*, pp. 143-63.

Spielberg, Steven (dir.) 1993, *Schindler's List*, Universal Pictures.

Stonebridge, Lyndsey 2007, *The Writing of Anxiety: Imagining Wartime in Mid-Century British Culture*, Palgrave Macmillan, London.

Street, Sarah 2009, *British National Cinema*, 2nd ed., Routledge, Abingdon.

Tan, Ed S. 1996, *Emotion and the Structure of Narrative Film: Film as an Emotion Machine*, Lawrence Erlbaum, Mahwah, NJ.

Toles, George 2013, 'Time's Timing and the Threat of Laughter in Nicolas Roeg's *Don't Look Now*', in Murray Pomerance (ed.), *The Last Laugh: Strange Humours of Cinema*, Wayne State University Press, Detroit, MI, pp. 109-26.

Towlson, Jon 2014, *Subversive Horror Cinema: Countercultural Messages of Films from Frankenstein to the Present*, McFarland, Jefferson, NC.

Trigg, Dylan 2009, 'The Place of Trauma: Memory, Hauntings, and the Temporality of Ruins', *Memory Studies*, vol. 2, no. 1, pp. 87-101.

--- 2006, *The Aesthetics of Decay: Nothingness, Nostalgia, and the Absence of Reason*, Peter Lang, New York.

Truffaut, François (dir.) 1966, *Fahrenheit 451*, Universal Pictures.

Tudor, Andrew 1989, *Monsters and Mad Scientists: A Cultural History of the Horror Movie*, Basil Blackwell, Oxford.

Uidhir, Christy Mag 2011, 'The Paradox of Suspense Realism', *Journal of Aesthetics and Art Criticism*, vol. 69, no. 2, pp. 161-71.

Visconti, Luchino (dir.) 1971, *Death in Venice*, Warner Bros.

von der Lippe, George 1999, 'Death in Venice in Literature and Film: Six 20th-Century Versions', *Mosaic*, vol. 32, no. 1, pp. 35-54.

Walker, Janet 2005, *Trauma Cinema: Documenting Incest and the Holocaust*, University of California Press, Berkeley.

Wallace, Diana 2004, 'Uncanny Stories: The Ghost Story as Female Gothic', *Gothic Studies*, vol. 6, no. 1, pp. 57-68.

Watkins, Elizabeth 2015, '*Don't Look Now*: Transience and Text', *Screen*, vol. 56, no. 4, pp. 436-49.

Watkins, Liz 2015, 'The Disquiet of the Everyday: Gesture and Bad Timing', *Journal for Cultural Research*, vol. 19, no. 1, pp. 56-68.

White, Rebecca 2016, 'Representations of Venice in Daphne Du Maurier's *Don't Look Now* and Nicolas Roeg's Screen Adaptation', in Michael O'Neill, Mark Sandy and Sarah Wootton (ed.), *Venice and the Cultural Imagination*, Routledge, Abingdon, pp. 157-72.

Whitford, Margaret 1991, *Luce Irigaray: Philosophy in the Feminine*, Routledge, London.

Williams, Tony 1996, *Hearths of Darkness: The Family in the American Horror Film*, Associated University Presses, Cranbury, NJ.

Wilson, Kristi 1999, 'Time, Space and Vision: Nicolas Roeg's *Don't Look Now*', *Screen*, vol. 40, no. 3, pp. 277-94.

Wisker, Gina 2013, 'Starting Your Journey in the Past, Speculating on Time and Place: Daphne Du Maurier's *The House on the Strand*, "Split Second", and the Engaged Fiction of Time Travel', *Journal of the Fantastic in the Arts*, vol. 24, no. 3, pp. 467-82.

--- 1999, '*Don't Look Now!* The Compulsions and Revelations of Daphne Du Maurier's Horror Writing', *Journal of Gender Studies*, vol. 8, no. 1, pp. 19-33.

Wood, Robin 2003, *Hollywood from Vietnam to Reagan ... And Beyond*, Exp. and rev. ed., Columbia University Press, New York.

--- 2002, 'The American Nightmare: Horror in the 70s', in Mark Jancovich (ed.), *Horror: The Film Reader*, Routledge, London, pp. 25-32.

Worland, Rick 2007, *The Horror Film: An Introduction*, Blackwell, Malden, MA.

Devil's Advocates

"Auteur Publishing's new Devil's Advocates critiques on individual titles offer bracingly fresh perspectives from passionate writers. The series will perfectly complement the BFI archive volumes." Christopher Fowler, Independent on Sunday

THE CURSE OF FRANKENSTEIN – MARCUS K. HARMES

"Harmes definitively establishes the decades-long impact of The Curse of Frankenstein on the gothic horror film genre."
Sydney Morning Herald

WITCHFINDER GENERAL – IAN COOPER

"I enjoyed it very much; it sets out all the various influences, both before and after the film, and indeed the essence of the film itself, very well indeed." Jonathan Rigby, author of English Gothic

THE DESCENT – JAMES MARRIOTT

"James Marriott makes a strong case for [The Descent] being the finest example of the films that revitalised the genre in the early years of the new millennium..." Black Static

BLACK SUNDAY – MARTYN CONTERIO

"Throughout, Conterio's approach, while immensely in-depth, is conversational in tone and very accessible... this monograph is an invaluable read for anyone with an interest, not only in Bava's work, but in the history of Italian horror cinema. Essential." Exquisite Terror

www.ingramcontent.com/pod-product-compliance
Lightning Source LLC
Chambersburg PA
CBHW071851230426
43671CB00012B/2149